TREASURER'S HANDBOOK

An introduction to voluntary sector finance and accounting

Gareth G Morgan

DIRECTORY OF SOCIAL CHANGE

Published by
The Directory of Social Change
24 Stephenson Way
London NW1 2DP
Tel: 020 7209 5151, fax: 020 7391 4804
e-mail: info@dsc.org.uk
from whom further copies and a full publications list are available.

The Directory of Social Change is a Registered Charity no. 800517

First published 2002

ISBN 1 900360 89 6

British Library Cataloguing in Publication Data
A catalogue record for this book is available from the British Library

Text and cover designed by Sarah Nicholson
Typeset, printed and bound by Stephen Austin, Hertford

Other Directory of Social Change departments in London:
Courses and conferences tel: 020 7209 4949
Charityfair/Charity Centre tel: 020 7209 1015
Publicity tel: 020 7391 4900
Research tel: 020 7391 4880

Directory of Social Change Northern Office:
Federation House, Hope Street, Liverpool L1 9BW
Courses and conferences tel: 0151 708 0117
Research tel: 0151 708 0136

Disclaimer
This is an introductory book. It seeks to explain the framework of charity accounting, but it does not provide a full statement of the law, nor does it fully reflect changes after 1 December 2001. Many accounting concepts are presented at an overview level only (particularly in areas such as accruals accounting, charity taxation, and production of final accounts). It is thus intended for guidance and is not a substitute for professional advice. No responsibility can be accepted by the publishers and author as a result of any person acting or refraining from acting on the basis of this publication.

Contents

About the series

Series editor: Alison Baxter

This book is part of a series of starter guides aimed primarily at those who are new to the voluntary sector. The series is designed for people involved with charities or voluntary organisations or community groups of any size. All the titles offer practical, straightforward advice to enable readers to get the most out of their roles and responsibilities.

Also available in this series:
The Charity Trustee's Handbook
Mike Eastwood
2001

The Minute Taker's Handbook
Lee Comer and Paul Ticher
2002

For further information, please contact the Directory of Social Change (see page ii for details).

Preface

The aim of *The Charity Treasurer's Handbook* is to bring together many areas related to effective accounting and financial management in UK charitable organisations in a book short enough to be read in a few hours. The role of treasurer, bookkeeper or finance worker in a voluntary organisation can be a rewarding one if it enables the organisation to achieve its aims. It need not be daunting, but it does require an appreciation of those issues that make the finances of charitable organisations different from those of businesses.

The book will be useful to those with financial experience in other sectors who need a rapid overview of the accounting issues in a charity. It is also intended for students on courses in charity and voluntary sector management who need an appreciation of the requirements of financial management in the sector.

This book outlines some of the key issues of charity law that affect the work of treasurers and finance officers in smaller charities. It explains a range of terminology such as restricted funds and the implications of the Charities Statement of Recommended Practice (SORP). It offers guidelines for day to day accounting procedures, as well as for year end accounts. It provides advice on issues such as appointing an auditor or independent examiner, and on general principles of financial management in small to medium charities.

The approach does not seek to cover every issue in detail, but simply to give enough information for the reader to understand the main requirements. It is hoped that this will enable a charity to make sensible decisions and to enter into meaningful discussions when further guidance is needed. Where more detail is needed, the list of further reading may be helpful.

The focus is on charitable voluntary organisations in the UK with total incomes in the range £5,000 to £500,000, but larger and smaller groups will also find the book useful. A good deal of the content will also be relevant to voluntary organisations without charitable status. But as explained in chapter 1, the impact of the Charities Act 1993 means many voluntary organisations that do not think of themselves as charities are in fact charitable in law. So the principles of this book apply to nearly all voluntary organisations, other than political organisations and private clubs.

One of the difficulties of charity law arises from the different legal systems in the different countries of the United Kingdom. The book starts from the position in England and Wales, which has the most comprehensive rules, but where possible it seeks to highlight differences in Scotland and in Northern Ireland. However, changes in charity law are likely in Scotland (as a result of the CharityScotland proposals), and possibly also in Northern Ireland. Legal and similar issues are stated in terms of the position as at 1 December 2001. But a book of this kind can give only an overview of legal issues – there are often more detailed requirements, exceptions and special cases that cannot be covered here. If in any doubt, it is often wise to take professional advice.

The book's central message is that being a charity treasurer or finance officer is an important and worthwhile role. It involves much more than keeping the books: the treasurer or finance officer is a key person in all kinds of strategic decisions and in ensuring the organisation meets the requirements of charity law. Contrary to popular belief, the role does not require massive accounting knowledge, nor a brilliant head for figures; all that is needed is a commitment to the importance of financial resources and a willingness to see them used effectively for the purposes of the charity.

Acknowledgements

I have been enormously privileged to work with several hundred charitable organisations in terms of their accounting and financial arrangements, in many cases helping them to implement procedures to reflect the new charity accounting rules and in some cases acting as their independent examiner. Others have attended training courses I presented, and raised significant questions, which have caused me to reflect. Many of the ideas in this book derive from the insights of those organisations, and I would like to dedicate the book to them.

I am also very appreciative of many individuals who have offered advice, listened to my questions and been willing to debate different approaches to charity accounting, especially at events such as the annual Charity Accountants Conference. This includes key figures in the Charity Commission, senior charity accountants, academic colleagues, members of the Council of the Association of Charity Independent Examiners and students on my courses.

I am also most grateful to the Directory of Social Change for inviting me to produce a book on this topic, and for the support of their Publishing Manager, Alison Baxter.

On a practical level, my wife Sharon, who is also my partner in Kubernesis, has given a great deal of encouragement to this project and agreed to the inclusion of certain Kubernesis materials. One of my administrators, Serena Ayre, kindly proof read the drafts of the whole book and contributed many helpful comments.

Nevertheless, I must stress that all opinions expressed are my own (unless another source is mentioned) and any errors remain my responsibility.

Gareth G Morgan
York
September 2001

About the author

Dr Gareth Morgan is Senior Partner of the York-based charity consultants The Kubernesis Partnership, which supports a wide range of charitable organisations – through training courses, consultancy, and software – in the areas of accounting, financial management, fundraising, strategy and charity law. In 1999 he was appointed as the first General Secretary to the Association of Charity Independent Examiners. He also holds a part-time academic post at Sheffield Hallam University where he is involved in research and teaching on issues of charity finance, and is Director of the University's Voluntary Sector Research Group. He is a trustee of two charities, and over the years has served as treasurer to a number of charitable organisations.

Example Financial Reports

Most of the financial reports in this book (chapters 7 and 9) are based on reports produced by the Kubernesis Accounting System (©The Kubernesis Partnership), although they have been re-typeset for this publication and do not represent actual computer output.

Further details of this and other aspects of the author's work are available from:

The Kubernesis Partnership
36 Acomb Wood Drive, York YO24 2XN
Tel: 01904 788885
E-mail: info@kubernesis.co.uk
Website: www.kubernesis.co.uk

1 Finance in charities and voluntary organisations

Before taking on the role of being a treasurer or finance officer in a charity, you need to understand what is meant by a charity. Charitable status makes a huge difference to the needs for accounting and financial management. But many more organisations are charities than people often realise and, as we will see, the term 'charity' actually includes a very large part of the voluntary sector.

Many people think that 'charity' applies only to certain types of organisations with a particular legal form, and which are registered with the Charity Commission: this is quite wrong. There are many possible legal structures for a charity, and there are many organisations which in law are charities, even though they are not registered as such: churches are probably the largest such category. Also, many organisations are charitable companies, which means they are subject to both charity law and company law. The principles of being a charity treasurer, and most of the law on charity accounting, apply to almost all charitable organisations.

The voluntary sector

To understand charities, we need to begin with voluntary organisations as a whole. People often refer to voluntary or not-for-profit (NFP) organisations as the 'third sector'. This is in contrast to the other two sectors – the commercial sector (business organisations) where profit is the central aim, and the public sector (for example government, local authorities and the health service) which, although being not-for-profit, is part of the work of the state. It is best to use the term 'not-for-profit' since many businesses going through hard times are non-profit making in certain years.

The financial management of NFP organisations is obviously quite different from profit-making organisations: the central aims are usually concerned with providing services or making a difference to the world. It is not part of the aims of the third sector to make a profit, and certainly such organisations are non-profit-distributing – that is, if they do make a profit or surplus one year, it is retained to support the work of the organisation in future years, not distributed to owners or shareholders.

To most people the word 'profit' implies profits being taken out, so it is best to avoid this term in the NFP sector: occasionally you may want to talk about the profit on a certain activity, but you cannot meaningfully talk about the profit of a charity as a whole. If a charity's income exceeds its expenditure in a given year, we say it has made a 'surplus' (or a 'deficit' if the expenditure was more than the income). Of course the income and expenditure will never be exactly equal, and in most NFP organisations a small surplus one year will be balanced by a small deficit another year. Sometimes surpluses are needed for a few years to build up sufficient reserves (see chapter 4), but it can never be right for a charity to be making surpluses indefinitely, as it would mean substantial amounts of income were not being spent on the charity's objects. This is a big contrast to the commercial sector, where a profit is normally sought every year.

There are some similarities between the public sector and the third sector in terms of bidding for resources and managing budgets; the fundamental difference is that public sector organisations are under government direction (national or local), whereas organisations in the voluntary sector are regarded as independent and can set their own directions and priorities.

This does not mean voluntary organisations are totally free of government control: they must obviously obey the laws of the land (including a number of specific issues of charity law and general issues such as employment and health and safety law) and many voluntary organisations get at least part of their income from government, for example through grants or Gift Aid tax refunds on donations (see chapter 12). But at the end of the day, a third sector organisation is primarily accountable to its own stakeholders, for example its members, trustees and beneficiaries.

A relationship of trust

This independence also creates a special relationship with funders and donors: a relationship of trust. Much income to charities (and to many other voluntary organisations) relies on money that is given to the organisation. Few people would make donations to commercial businesses or to the public sector, but people routinely give to charities and to other third sector organisations without seeking anything in return other than an expectation that their gifts will be used to advance the aims of the organisation.

This does not just apply to personal donations; most grants, whether from the public sector or from other charities, are *given* to a charity. Grants and donations may be subject to specific conditions on the use of the money – this gives rise to restricted funds (see chapter 3) – but ultimately the relationship with the funder or donor is one in which money is given and the charity is entrusted with using it properly.

This is in complete contrast to commercial organisations, where most of the income is from sales, in which the relationship is contractual (for example 'We will let you have this tin of paint if you pay us £2.50'). Charities can also have contractual income – trading income (see chapter 11) – but for most charities, money that is given is their main source of income.

This relationship of trust is central to understanding voluntary sector finance, and is also the reason why much charity law is part of trust law. For this reason, those who have the day to day control of a charity (for example a management committee or church council) are called 'trustees': they are entrusted with funds given by others, to advance the charity's aims. However, the trust relationship can also apply elsewhere in the sector, for example with political trusts. Any grant or donation to a voluntary organisation implies some kind of trust relationship.

Trustees who fail to respect such relationships are guilty of a breach of trust, a serious matter that can result in court action. In extreme cases, a trustee who recklessly commits a breach of trust might have to reimburse the charity personally for money which was wrongly used.

In some NFP organisations it is common for board members to be paid – for example, in the public sector many people serving on trust boards are entitled to allowances or salaries. But a central issue of charity law is that charity trustees must be unpaid: they can, naturally, be reimbursed expenses, but the role of being a charity trustee is voluntary. This clearly includes the treasurer, since a charity treasurer is normally a key trustee (except in rare cases where someone takes on the treasurership without having the right to vote at trustees' meetings).

There are some exceptions to this rule in charities that have special governing instruments allowing certain trustees to be paid fees, and in other one-off cases a charity can apply for individual approval from the Charity Commission. But these are relatively rare, and in any case such payments are usually for professional services separate from the actual duties of being a trustee. Excluding these cases, paying anything to a trustee other than reimbursement of expenses is a clear breach of trust. As shown in chapter 7, to help safeguard against abuses, any payments to trustees must normally be shown separately in the charity's published accounts.

The principle of unpaid governance is at the heart of the voluntary sector, and even non-charitable voluntary organisations will find it hard to get grants if their committee members are paid. Some people question the term 'voluntary sector', pointing out that many charities nowadays do much of their work through paid staff, with limited use of volunteers. But all voluntary organisations rely on volunteers at the trustee level.

For more information on trusteeship, see the *Charity Trustee's Handbook*, also in this series.

What is a charity?

For any organisation to be a charity, it must clearly be a voluntary organisation, with a group of people – the trustees – responsible on an unpaid basis for deciding on the use of the funds (subject to any conditions imposed by donors).

But not all voluntary organisations are charities. However, the test of charitable status depends not on a certain structure nor on registration with the Charity Commission, but on two key tests:

- The organisation must have exclusively charitable objects. The definition of this goes back to a 1601 statute of Elizabeth I (as interpreted and extended by the Courts over the years). To be charitable, the objects of the organisation must fit entirely into one or more of the four 'heads of charity':

(a) the advancement of religion;
(b) the relief of poverty;
(c) the advancement of education;
(d) other purposes beneficial to community (as accepted by the Courts as being sufficiently close to the first three).

- The organisation must exist for public benefit. In other words, it must seek to benefit a wide range of people (and there must be no private benefit – for example, except in very exceptional cases, the trustees must be unpaid). With heads (a) to (c) the public benefit is generally presumed – for example, education is presumed to benefit society as a whole – but for charitable status to be agreed under head (d) the public benefit must be explicit.

Various changes to this law have been suggested, but in fact a very wide range of voluntary organisations seeking to do work that most people would regard as worthwhile can fit into one or more of these categories if they word their governing document appropriately. For example, organisations in the health field are accepted as charitable on the principle that relieving sickness reduces poverty. The fourth head includes the provision of facilities for welfare and leisure time occupation (which covers most community associations) as well as newer areas such as the promotion of race relations and the promotion of urban or rural regeneration. Some umbrella charities, such as councils for voluntary service, have objects concerned with improving the effectiveness of other charities, which thus potentially advances all four heads.

These principles of charitable status apply throughout the UK, and in many other countries whose legal system derives from the UK. In England and Wales the decision on whether a particular organisation meets the criteria for charitable status is made by the Charity Commission, although in theory an appeal to the Courts is possible. Elsewhere the Inland Revenue is currently the main day to day interpreter of the law, in deciding whether an organisation is entitled to charitable tax concessions.

It follows that the governing document of the charity (its constitution, memorandum and articles of association, trust deed, or rules – see *Legal forms*, page 6) is vital in determining charitable status, in particular the objects of the organisation, and the range of beneficiaries will be central to this. In theory it is possible to have a charity without a written constitution – occasionally people make the mistake of launching major appeals without any written documents; in such cases the charitable status of the funds raised would depend on witnesses testifying to what had been said at the time. But in the long term it is very hard to raise funds without a formal structure.

In practice, the main voluntary organisations excluded from charitable status tend to be:

- those whose aims are deemed in law to be at least partly political – for example, campaigning organisations whose main aim is to achieve a change in the law;
- those not offering sufficient public benefit – for example a tenants group working purely with the tenants in a given block of flats or a club whose facilities are only available to its members (unless the membership rules make it easy for anyone to join).

Unless your organisation is clearly excluded from charitable status, it is safest to work on the assumption that it is a charity, until proven otherwise. This means producing accounts to comply with charity law and, in England and Wales, the trustees must apply for the charity to be registered unless it is clearly excepted or exempt (see *Charitable status*, page 9). (You won't qualify for charity tax concessions unless your charitable status is clearly established.)

As a charity treasurer or finance officer, you do not need to be an expert on charitable status, but you do need to understand the basic framework for your organisation's status, and you must certainly be aware of its charitable objects as stated in the governing document. See *Further reading* for sources of further information.

Legal forms

Charities can have one of a number of legal structures; once you have a copy of your governing document it should be clear which structure applies. Table 1.1 shows most of the main structures.

The vast majority of new charities are established using one of the first three structures; if you are taking over in a long established organisation, the other forms can arise.

To form a new charity, a charitable trust is the simplest structure: you simply need someone to make an initial donation (the 'settlor') and by means of a trust deed the objects are defined and initial trustees appointed. Most grant-making charities use this structure.

Table 1.1 Legal structures

Legal form	Governing document	Usual internal term for trustees
Charitable trust	Trust deed	Trustees
Charitable association	Constitution	Committee
Charitable company	Memorandum and articles (company limited by guarantee)	Directors or board members
Industrial and provident society (working for the benefit of the community)	Rules	Committee
Charities established by Royal Charter (for example Scouts/Guides and certain professional bodies)	Charter	Council
Charities established by Act of Parliament (for example most Church of England bodies)	Act of Parliament (or regulations made under the Act)	Various terms

For a more democratic structure, with members electing a committee to act as trustees, the charitable association is the easiest model. Essentially, a group of people with common interests agree to associate themselves together, and agree to a constitution or set of rules that determines the criteria for membership and the procedures for electing the committee. A wide range of local community-based charities and service-providing organisations use this structure. But it is vital to keep proper records, to distinguish between ordinary members of the association (who have the right to vote at the AGM) and members of the committee (who have day to day control of funds are thus the trustees of the charity).

A charitable company has the advantage of being a legally separate 'incorporated' entity: this means, for example, if the charity needs to purchase freehold property it can be registered in the name of the charity, rather than in the names of individual trustees. Also, if the charity enters into a contract that goes wrong, and the charity finds itself being sued, the rules of limited liability apply, i.e. the charity's own resources could be lost in a court action, but the trustees could not be sued personally for breach of contract. In unincorporated charities, such as trusts and associations, the trustees could in theory be personally liable if things go badly wrong.

However, many people exaggerate the benefits of limited liability. In the first place, the protections of limited liability apply only if the directors/trustees have complied with all the requirements of company law. This gives a vast range of legal responsibilities over and above the requirements of charity law so, for example, unless you know what is meant in company law by 'wrongful trading' and how to avoid it, limited liability is of little help. Also, limited liability is only relevant in contract law; if, for example, you misuse restricted funds, that is a breach of trust. Thirdly, many risks can be mitigated in all types of charities by appropriate insurance: for example, charities giving advice certainly need professional indemnity insurance. Allowing the whole charity to collapse because of one disgruntled person taking legal action is hardly a good strategy in the first place: limited liability might protect the trustees, but staff would lose their jobs and other beneficiaries would lose out. Finally, it has to be said that it is very rare for charity trustees acting in good faith to find themselves facing legal action; the bad publicity that would arise from suing a group of volunteers will put most people off.

A new legal structure has been widely recommended by various reports, to be known as a charitable incorporated organisation (CIO) – this would be governed purely by charity law but would be an incorporated body with limited liability – thus giving most of the benefits of the charitable company without all the additional requirements of company law. However, new primary legislation is needed before this becomes possible, so in the meantime, charities will need to choose between the structures above.

As a treasurer or finance officer, you need to be clear what structure you are accounting for. If your organisation is a charitable company, your accounting procedures must comply with company law as well as charity law; a number of differences are highlighted in the following chapters.

Subsidiary groups

Another vital issue on the legal structure, which is often overlooked, is to be clear on the boundaries of your organisation: as treasurer, you need some control over *all* the finances of the charity that are in any way managed by your trustees. If you have several funds or projects, your accounts must reflect them all. Furthermore, many charities have groups that run their own finances, but which see themselves as part of the main charity. For example, a community association may run an older people's support group, and may have an arts and drama club meeting on its premises. As treasurer, you must be clear whether each such group is:

- legally part of your charity – if so, its work is under the control of the charity's trustees, and its finances must be included in the published accounts of the charity; or
- an independent organisation simply using your premises – if so, it must not attempt to use your charity registration number, and if its income is over £1,000 it will normally need to be registered as a charity in its own right.

This is also important when charities hand out funds to local groups. If you give money to independent groups, there must be a clear point when the grant ceases to be in the funds of your charity and control passes to the separate group. But if the main charity passes money to a group which is still legally part of that charity, your accounts will simply show a transfer between funds: no money has gone out of the charity as a whole.

Charitable status

As explained above, many different organisations can be charities, and not all charities are registered. In fact, at present the concept of registered charities only applies in England and Wales. There are currently five forms of charitable status recognised in the United Kingdom:

- *Exempt charities* (England and Wales) – these are a small number of bodies listed in Schedule 2 of the Charities Act 1993 – they are mainly large national bodies under other laws, although industrial and provident societies are included. Most parts of the Charities Act 1993 do not apply but the Charities SORP (see chapter 2) is still the normal basis for presenting the accounts, unless other legislation overrides this.
- *Excepted charities* (England and Wales) – these are excepted from registration under s3(5) of the Charities Act 1993 but they are still subject to other aspects of the Act, including the accounting rules. The main examples are:

(a) charities with less than £1,000 income and no permanent endowment or occupation of land;
(b) registered places of worship (buildings registered with the local authority as, for example, a church, mosque or synagogue);
(c) other charities excepted by Regulations – this includes many other religious charities and charities for the upkeep of graves. However, the government is consulting on possible changes to these regulations, to take effect after September 2002.

- *Registered charities* – all other charities in England and Wales must be registered by the Charity Commission, and are given a 'registered charity number', which must appear on many documents, including cheques, invoices, receipts and bills.
- *Scottish charities* – these are currently recognised by the Scottish Inland Revenue and are given a Scottish charity number beginning 'SC'.
- *Northern Ireland charities* – charitable status is less clearly regulated in Northern Ireland, and decisions on charitable status for tax purposes are made by the Inland Revenue.

It should be noted that all these are charities in law: they all have exactly the same tax concessions and other privileges of charitable status. If a charity's work spreads across several countries of the UK, its location for charity law is normally determined by the location of the majority of the trustees.

It is also vital to appreciate that charitable status is not an optional 'badge'. In England and Wales, it is compulsory under s3 of the Charities Act 1993 for the trustees of a charitable organisation to apply for registration unless it is clearly exempted or excepted (and they are committing an offence if they fail to do so). It follows that, apart from places of worship, most other voluntary organisations in England and Wales with an income of £1,000 or more need to apply for registration as charities unless their aims or benefits are clearly non-charitable.

In the case of a company limited by guarantee, the company registration (with Companies House) and charity registration (with the Charity Commission) are completely separate; the charity must report each year to both regulators.

The Charity Commission

In England and Wales, much of the regulation of charities, and many of the requirements for charity accounting – such as convening the SORP Committee – are handled through the Charity Commission. The Commission has various powers defined by the Charities Act 1993; it is a government department, but independent of direct day to day government control. All registered charities have to complete an annual form for the Commission, and the Commissioners have great powers to intervene to protect charitable funds where abuse appears to be taking place.

Some charity treasurers mistakenly feel their task is largely about keeping the Charity Commission happy. This is misleading – the Commission's requirements are only one small part of a treasurer's role – but as a charity treasurer, you will need to ensure that your accounts are sent to the Commission each year, and you will probably be responsible for completing much of the annual return. However, you will also find the Commission a helpful source of information and guidance, particularly in terms of publications – see *Further reading* for more details.

If you are a treasurer of an excepted charity – such as a place of worship – you do not normally have to send accounts to the Charity Commission every year. But your charity is still subject to the Charities Act accounting provisions and almost all the Commission's guidance materials are just as relevant as for registered charities. The Charity Commission has the same powers to take action if it believes charitable funds are at risk.

The McFadden report in Scotland has proposed the creation of a body called CharityScotland, which would have many similar powers to the Charity Commission in England and Wales. Progress towards this depends on legislation in the Scottish Parliament.

2 Accounts at different levels: the legal requirements

When someone asks to look at your accounts, this can mean many different things. The term 'accounts' can cover anything from the detailed books and records to the final published accounts, and anything in between.

Levels of detail

For most charities, accounts will work at three levels of detail – see table 2.1.

The accounts start with the basic books of the charity, where every transaction – every receipt, payment or other entry – is recorded individually. The formal term for these is your *accounting records*. As a treasurer or finance officer, you must ensure books are kept up to date with all the relevant entries – chapter 5 explores ways of handling the bookkeeping. The books are the starting point for all other financial analysis.

This is a fundamental difference between charity accounting and personal accounting. With your personal household accounts you can, if you choose, just look at your bank balance and count the cash in your purse or wallet without ever recording the actual income and expenditure. In fact, even some self-employed business people manage to work with minimal records (although this can make it hard to justify profit figures to the Inland Revenue). But in a charity, the trustees are handling other people's money, and you have both a legal and a moral obligation to keep detailed records of the income as it comes in, and exactly how it is spent.

Table 2.1 Accounting levels

Concept	*Official term*
THE BOOKS Records of all transactions. Must show the financial position of the charity at any time and be kept for six years. Must be seen by an auditor or independent examiner – otherwise for internal use only.	**Accounting records**
INTERIM REPORTS Typically reports for trustees or key members of staff to monitor progress and take financial decisions. Will not usually show individual transactions, but generally summarise figures for a period of less than a year. May show actuals against budgets and possibly future projections. For internal use only.	**Management accounts**
PUBLISHED YEAR END ACCOUNTS Show financial position of whole charity. All charities, no matter how small, must produce published accounts, which must be approved by the trustees. Includes report by an auditor or independent examiner (unless under £10,000 income). The annual accounts should always be circulated with the annual report. They are a public document – anyone can ask for a copy.	**Financial statements** or **annual accounts** or just **the accounts**

However, if you have more than about 20 or 30 transactions, it is difficult for anyone to get an idea of how the charity is doing just by looking at the books. You need some means of summarising the records into a form that will be meaningful for taking decisions. Such internal summaries of the books are called *management accounts*. Normally they will show the total income and expenditure under headings such as 'donations, sales, bank interest' and 'salaries, premises, printing' and so on rather than listing every transaction. If you have several funds or projects (see chapter 3) the management accounts will also be broken down by fund. Where budgets have been agreed, management accounts are often presented showing actual figures compared with budgets (see chapter 9).

One of the important tasks of the treasurer or finance officer is to produce regular management accounts for the trustees. In a small charity this may be just a one page summary, but regular meaningful financial information is essential for decision making.

The third level is the final year end published accounts – the *annual accounts* – see chapter 7. One of the conditions of charitable status is that your organisation must, once a year, make available a full set of accounts reporting the income and expenditure for the year, the balances at year end, and the different funds involved. These must be sent to the Charity Commission if your organisation is a registered charity but, more importantly, copies must be made available to anyone on request (you can make a small charge to cover copying and postage if necessary). Different formats apply to different sizes of charity, but even a tiny charity with only £100 per year income must still produce published accounts – there is no such thing as a secret charity.

The books and management accounts will normally be the responsibility of the treasurer and any staff with finance roles. As treasurer or finance officer, you may have the task of drafting the final accounts, but they must be approved by the trustees as a whole. However, approving the published accounts is one of the key actions of the trustees as a whole in taking responsibility for the affairs of the charity.

The legal framework and the SORP

Charity accounts are governed extensively by law, as summarised in table 2.2. In most respects, the rules on charity accounting are more extensive than those for commercial accounts: this is because charities are entrusted with other people's money and have a duty to use those funds for public benefit. Charity accounting requirements have changed enormously since the early-1990s: even many professional accountants, if they are not charity specialists, may be unaware of the full implications.

In England and Wales, most current charity law comes from the Charities Act 1993 which, either directly or by Regulations, gives considerable detail on what a charity must do in terms of accounting. In Scotland, the rules currently depend on 1992 Regulations; however, it is expected that before long the Scottish Parliament will enact new legislation as part of the CharityScotland proposals, which is likely to bring Scottish charities closer to those in England and Wales. In Northern Ireland, the requirements currently derive from the Charities Act (Northern Ireland) 1964, although changes have been proposed, which again are likely to be closer to England and Wales.

Table 2.2 The basis of the law on charity accounting

England and Wales

- Charities Act 1993 (Part VI)
- Charities (Accounts and Reports) Regulations 1995 and 2000
- Charities SORP (see below)
- Charity Commission Directions and Guidance (in some areas these have the force of law, especially the Directions to Independent Examiners)

Scotland

- Law Reform (Miscellaneous Provisions) (Scotland) Act 1990 s4&5
- Charities Accounts (Scotland) Regulations 1992
- Charities SORP (see below)

Northern Ireland

- Charities Act (Northern Ireland) 1964
- Charities SORP (see below)

The Charities SORP

- Statement of Recommended Practice on Accounting and Reporting by Charities
  Published by the Charity Commission with approval by the Accounting Standards Board (revised SORP October 2000). The SORP applies throughout the British Isles (including Scotland and the whole of Ireland – north and south). It applies to all charities, including charitable companies.

See *Further reading* for sources of these documents

However, in all parts of the UK, a major addition to the framework comes from the *Statement of Recommended Practice on Accounting and Reporting by Charities* usually abbreviated to the 'Charities SORP' or just 'SORP'. In practice, people often talk about the whole regime as the SORP, as in the question 'Are your accounts SORP-compliant?'.

You might think that, as the title includes the word 'recommended', you can ignore the SORP if you wish, but in fact it is compulsory in many cases. Any accounts designed to give a 'true and fair view' should comply with relevant accounting standards (for example, with charitable companies, this is a requirement of the Companies Acts) and if the organisation is a charity, the SORP is certainly relevant. Secondly, in England and Wales, the Charity Commission has stated that it 'expects the accounts of charities and their accounting practices to comply fully with the SORP' and may well use its powers to institute inquiries if not. Thirdly, the Regulations in England and Wales are drafted with extensive references to the SORP and, furthermore, for a charity whose income is over £250,000, any departures from the SORP must be disclosed by specific notes to the accounts. Finally, most funders nowadays expect SORP-compliant accounts, at least for charities over £100,000 income, and sometimes below this.

So, except for small charities just using receipts and payments accounts (see *Accruals or receipts and payments*, page 20), you ignore the SORP at your peril – and in fact, even for receipts and payments, the SORP includes several pages of useful advice.

Thus, in each regime the rules are based on a combination of primary legislation (Acts of Parliament), secondary legislation (Regulations issued as Statutory Instruments) and other standards such as the SORP. But although charity treasurers need an overview of the rules, this book is not attempting to cover the full detail (for more information see *Further reading*). In general, the rules for England and Wales are the most comprehensive, and with the various regimes likely to come closer with future legislation, this book will focus on the rules for England and Wales, highlighting differences in Scotland and Northern Ireland only where they are fundamental.

In some charities there may be additional rules imposed by parent bodies. For example, many national charities with independent local branches require certain information to be shown in the branch accounts as a condition of belonging to the national body or to comply with other legislation, for example the Church Accounting Regulations in the Church of England. But such rules are always additional to the main regime; they cannot override the SORP or relax rules required by law.

What does the law require?

Referring back to the three levels of accounts, in relation to the *books*, the law requires that all charities must keep proper accounting records 'sufficient to disclose, with reasonable accuracy, the financial position of the charity' at any time. They must also be sufficient to allow the production of proper accounts at year end.

It follows that what is sometimes called 'shoebox accounting', where the treasurer or bookkeeper throws everything in a box and hopes someone else will sort it out at year end, is not only unwise, it is actually illegal! With a shoebox approach there will be many times when the financial position cannot be ascertained.

The law also requires that the records must be kept for six years from the end of the year concerned. If there are changes of treasurer, be sure that the last six years' books and papers are passed on and not destroyed. Also remember that the full records include the bills and vouchers – not just the entries in the books.

However, the law does not prescribe *how* the books are to be kept. You are free to use any method of bookkeeping, manual or computerised, that will enable the charity to comply with the overall requirements. With computer systems, ensure you have full printouts at year end. Although large organisations sometimes dispense with paper records, for a small charity it is risky to rely on six year old computer backups, given the rate of change of hardware and software.

Remember, too, that the full accounting records may be divided between several sets of books or computer systems. If you have staff, your payroll records are part of the books of the charity. If you have people giving individual donations – for example under a Gift Aid scheme – it is unlikely that your main books will show every separate gift, particularly where donors are giving weekly or monthly, so your fundraising records must also be retained. (The need for donor confidentiality does not replace the need for proper records.)

At the second level, the *management accounts*, there are no specific legal requirements. The trustees have a duty to manage the charity properly and, except in a tiny organisation, this will mean monitoring the finances more than once a year, so some kind of interim financial reports are essential (see chapter 9). However, it is for the trustees of each charity to decide what is appropriate.

Most of the law on charity accounting relates to the final level, the published *annual accounts* – references in law to the 'accounts' of a charity mean the published year end accounts. Much of the Regulations and SORP are concerned with the final accounts; chapter 7 outlines some of the steps involved. However, the rules sensibly recognise that a small local charity cannot be expected to produce the same sort of annual accounts as a large national organisation, so the regime has a series of thresholds.

The thresholds

Much of the charity accounting regime is determined by the total income of the charity. For smaller charities, the regime is not particularly onerous; as a charity grows in income, the rules become more demanding. But it is vital to appreciate that all charities, no matter how small, are affected by some rules: occasionally one hears people saying 'I don't need to bother about the Charities Act because our income is under £100,000' – unfortunately this is a serious misunderstanding.

Table 2.3 shows the main accounting requirements for unincorporated charities in England and Wales (that is, charities which are not companies). Each level shows the additional requirements; the requirements at the lower levels also apply.

The thresholds are based on the total income of the charity, considering all funds and projects together (even if some keep their own books). Some of the thresholds are also affected by expenditure levels and by figures from prior years. So to be certain, a charity should work on the largest income or expenditure for any of the last three years.

Note that these are *minimum* requirements at each level. A charity is free to do more if it wishes. For example, a charity with income around £60,000 that is bidding for a grant which would take it over £100,000 may well find that producing full SORP-compliant accounts even at the current income level helps demonstrate that it has the professionalism to expand.

The main difference for charitable companies is that there is no provision for receipts and payments accounts; accruals accounts (see below) must be produced no matter how small the income. There are also differences in the rules for scrutiny of the accounts, as explained in chapter 8.

For unincorporated charities in Scotland, the thresholds are mostly one step down, i.e. accruals accounts are required if the income exceeds £25,000, and an audit (rather than independent examination) begins at £100,000 income, though, as explained, this is under review by the Scottish Parliament. In Northern Ireland, as yet there are no specific thresholds enshrined in legislation, but working at least to the thresholds for England and Wales is a way of demonstrating good practice.

Table 2.3 Minimum accounting requirements (Unincorporated charities in England and Wales)

Income	Minimum requirements
All charities	Must keep proper accounting records (retained for six years).
	Must produce an annual report and accounts (the accounts can be on a receipts and payments basis).
	Must provide accounts to the Charity Commission if requested and to members of the public on request.
> £1,000	Must apply to become a registered charity (unless exempt or excepted). If registered, must complete the Charity Commission annual Database Update.
> £10,000	Registered charity status must be shown on documents including cheques and appeals (unless exempt or excepted).
	Accounts must be independently examined or audited (see chapter 8).
	Annual report and accounts must be sent to Charity Commission and must complete Charity Commission Annual Return.
> £100,000	Full accruals accounting required and presentation of accounts must comply with Regulations with SOFA, balance sheet and notes (SORP format).
> £250,000	Full audit compulsory.
	Accounts must specifically disclose any departures from the SORP.
> £2.8 million	Accounts must included cashflow statement.

See the text for explanation of terms used in this table.

Accruals or receipts and payments?

In terms of producing the accounts, the biggest difference is whether to produce accounts on a receipts and payments basis or on an accruals basis. In England and Wales, the receipts and payments basis is allowed up to £100,000 income (for charities which are not companies); above this accruals accounts are compulsory.

It is vital to note that whether you use receipts and payments or accruals, the law has requirements about the presentation of the accounts. For example, even if the income of the charity is below £100,000, you must either produce receipts and payments accounts complying with the Charities Act, or accruals accounts complying with the Act, Regulations and SORP.

In either case, there are two main reports, showing: what has come into and gone out of the charity over the year (a 'movements' report), and what is in hand at year end (a 'snapshot' report). The basic requirements are described below – see chapter 7 for further details.

- Receipts and payments accounting
  (a) receipts and payments account (broken down by funds);
  (b) statement of assets and liabilities (the 'SOAL').
- Accruals accounting
  (a) statement of financial activities (the 'SOFA');
  (b) balance sheet;
  (c) notes to the accounts.

The SOFA was invented specifically for charity accounting: it is basically an income and expenditure account, divided into columns for the different types of funds. (The funds are explained in chapter 3, and an example SOFA appears in figure 7.2.) Once people get used to the SOFA they usually find it very helpful in getting a picture of a whole charity. The layout of a charity's SOFA, balance sheet, and the various information needed in the notes are covered in some detail in the Regulations and SORP.

With receipts and payments accounts, the rules are less detailed: provided the different funds are clearly separated, the presentation of the year's receipts and payments is quite flexible. But although you don't have to do a full balance sheet with receipts and payments accounts, the charity must be able to produce a list of its assets (things the charity has, for example money in the bank or items of equipment) and liabilities at year end (for example unpaid bills): hence the need for the SOAL.

Accountants often regard receipts and payments accounting and accruals accounting as distinct worlds, but in a charity many normal transactions such as receiving a donation or paying wages will be treated the same in either case. The main differences relate to debtors, creditors and fixed assets.

For example, suppose your charity rents out rooms to other organisations, and had raised a substantial bill for room hire that has not been paid by the year end of 31 March 2003 – this would constitute a debtor in the year end accounts. With receipts and payments accounts, you would simply list the debtor on your SOAL in the 2002/03 accounts, but you wouldn't actually record a receipt until the following year (2003/04) ,when you were paid.

But with accruals accounts, you would say 'this rent was income earned by the charity in the year 2002/03, and it should thus be included as part of the charity's income on the SOFA for that year' (balanced by a debtor on the balance sheet – because at that stage the money is not in the bank). Then in 2003/04, when the room rents are paid, you would just make a transfer from debtors to bank – you wouldn't show any new income, as the income had already been recorded in 2002/03 (or, to use accountants' language, the income was 'recognised' in the earlier year).

If your charity has incurred significant expenses during the year that have not been paid at year end, you would record a year end creditor on the same lines, using the receipts and payments or accruals approach as relevant.

Tangible fixed assets are items expected to last several years – for example, buildings, computers or vehicles. With receipts and payments accounting, you would record the whole cost of such an item at the time of purchase (and list it on the SOAL for as long as it was kept). But with accruals accounting, you would show the item on the balance sheet and then *depreciate* it over several years. So on each year's SOFA, only that year's depreciation appears as expenditure, and the cost is thus spread over the expected life of the item.

The idea with accruals accounting is that the accounts are more likely to show a 'true and fair view' of the income that has 'accrued' to the charity for the year and of the expenses incurred in running the charity. Occasionally, if there are few debtors, creditors or fixed assets, the figures will be almost the same whether you use receipts and payments or accruals. But receipts and payments accounts can sometimes show huge fluctuations from year to year: for example if a grant was paid just before year end one year, and just after year end in the following year, or if one year included the purchase of a large fixed asset. Obviously accruals accounting means a little more work, but it allows much more meaningful comparisons to be made from year to year.

If your income is £100,000 or over (£25,000 in Scotland) or if your charity is a company, you have no choice, and you must use accruals accounts, with the full SORP-format for your final accounts (SOFA etc).

Below this limit you have a choice between receipts and payments or accruals, but it is best to be consistent for a number of years. Remember the choice affects both:

- how you record certain transactions (where debtors, creditors or fixed assets are involved); and
- the format in which the final accounts are presented.

Issues of accruals accounting are considered further in chapter 10.

3 Charitable funds

If you were keeping the accounts of a business, apart from certain special professions, you would have just one fund: the profit and loss account. All sales income goes into, and all business expenses are charged to the profit and loss account. Larger businesses may choose to divide the profit and loss into departments, each with their own cost codes, so they can measure the profitability of each area – but this is purely a matter of internal management. At the end of the year, the profits are added together because they all belong to the same owners or shareholders.

In a charity, things can be very different. Most charities start with one fund – usually called the general fund – which receives donations, and from which the expenses of the charity are paid – and the report of this fund forms an income and expenditure account (or a receipts and payments account if you are using receipts and payments accounting). At the level of management accounts, the income and expenditure account in a not-for-profit organisation is equivalent to the profit and loss account in a business.

But before long, the chances are that the charity will have a special appeal (say, for building renovations) or will want to launch a new project, and will start to seek funding specifically for that work.

If this is successful, and grants or donations are received specifically for the new project, then of course the relationship of trust (explained in chapter 1) means that the trustees must ensure money given for the new project is only spent on the purposes for which it was given. This requires careful bookkeeping, because clearly the new project needs its own income and expenditure account, separate from the income and expenditure account of the general fund, otherwise there is no way of tracking whether money received for the new project is really spent on the purposes intended.

The new project thus needs to be treated as a separate fund in the accounts – a *restricted fund* – because there are restrictions on how it can be used. If money given for the new roof appeal were spent on the general running costs of the charity, those who had given to the new appeal (whether they were individuals or big grantmakers) would rightly be concerned; they could ask for their money back, and the trustees would be guilty of a breach of trust.

Sooner or later, other special projects and appeals will come along, each of which needs its own restricted fund if it is supported by grants or donations given specifically for that purpose. Even very straightforward local organisations will often have two or three funds; large charities can sometimes find themselves managing hundreds of funds.

What is a fund?

A fund is essentially a 'pot' of money or resources held for specific purposes.

As explained, most charities will have a general fund which can be used for any purpose so long as it is within the charity's overall objects – this is known as an *unrestricted fund* – i.e. there are no external restrictions on it (apart from the requirement that all the funds of the charity must be used to support the charity's objects).

Restricted funds are 'pots' of money or resources where there is some external condition on how the fund can be used. The condition could arise in one of two ways:

- from the way you asked for the money in the first place (as in 'please give to our new roof appeal'); or
- from a condition imposed by a funder or donor (as in 'this grant must only be used for the salary of the outreach worker').

Many people use some measure of fund accounting for their personal household finances: if you put aside money into different jars (or different bank accounts) labelled 'holiday money' or 'children's clothes' you are actually doing fund accounting. In this case, the funds would be classed as *designated* funds, because you have decided to designate each jar for a certain purpose, however, you could in principle raid your holiday fund for another purpose if there was something more urgent. Designated funds, like general funds, are part of the general class of unrestricted funds. But, on the other hand, if someone else has made a condition – for example if your aunt gave you a cheque for your birthday and said 'I want you to spend this on some nice new clothes' then it would be a restricted fund – spending it on something else would be a breach of trust between you and your aunt!

Quite often charities will want to set aside some money from general funds into a designated fund – for example, many charities with buildings to maintain have a 'repairs fund' and every year make a transfer from the general fund to the repairs fund. Then, when a major repair arises, hopefully they have enough in the repairs fund to cover the cost, even though it may be more than they could afford in a single year.

The difference between a designated fund and a restricted fund depends on how the fund came to be set up. If it was an internal decision by the charity trustees to set aside the money, then it is a designated fund. If necessary, your trustees could decide the money was more urgently needed for something else. But if the money was externally given on specific conditions, you cannot use it for something else without getting permission from the donor(s) or funder(s) concerned.

This has implications for fundraising – see chapter 12. Obviously people will often give more generously if they know their money will be used for a specific purpose, and some funders such as the National Lottery distributors will only support specific projects, so their grants are always restricted (except perhaps with a start-up grant for a new organisation). But if you allow fundraisers to offer a slightly different project to every supporter, it can become almost impossible to track all the separate funds involved.

There is a further type of fund only found in certain charities, known as a *capital fund* or *endowment fund*. This is even more restricted: capital (or endowment) funds arise when someone gives money to the charity and says 'I want you to invest this, and use the income for certain purposes, but you mustn't actually spend the capital'. Many grant-making charities derive most of their resources from capital funds set up by someone who wanted to create a long term resource that could continue making grants long after their death. But sometimes charities will appeal specifically for an endowment fund: for example, charities raising money for specialist medical equipment often have to raise an endowment fund to provide for the running costs of the equipment. (The terms 'capital fund' and 'endowment fund' mean the same thing, but 'endowment' is usually used where long term investments are involved.)

In such cases, the income of the capital fund – for example interest or share dividends – is posted to another fund (either restricted or unrestricted) so that the income can be spent on the required purpose. But the value of the capital fund itself can go up or down if the assets in the fund (e.g. shares) change value over the year.

With receipts and payments accounting, the balance of a fund is just the money in the fund. But with accruals accounting, any fund can comprise a mixture of money and/or other assets and liabilities. So, even if you do not have any endowment funds in the investment sense, you may still need to show capital funds in your accounts if, for example, you received a capital grant to purchase a new building: the balance of the fund would be the value of the building.

Figure 3.1 shows the different types of funds in the way they are classified by the SORP. Strictly speaking, a normal restricted fund where the income can be spent (within the terms of the restriction) should be called a *restricted income* fund.

Figure 3.1 Types of fund

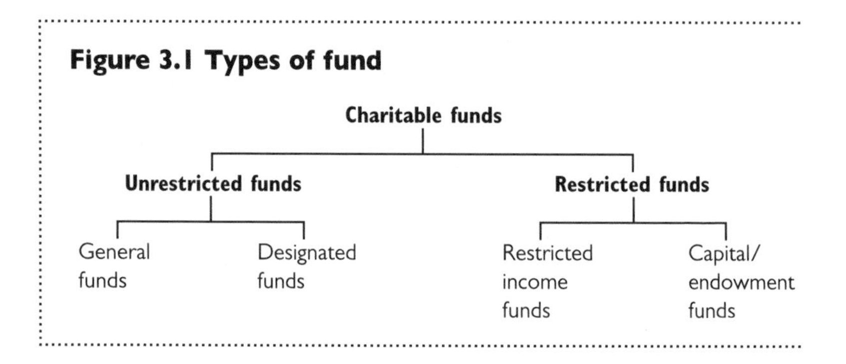

Multi-fund accounting

The need to account for a number of separate funds is probably the biggest issue that distinguishes charity accounting from business accounting.

You may find, for example, that you need many more categories for income and expenditure than you initially thought. It is no good having just one income category for donations: you need to distinguish general (unrestricted) donations, donations for the new roof fund, donations for the outreach fund, and so on. On the expenditure side, if you have staff working on different projects with separate funders, it is no good having one expenditure category for salaries, you need to distinguish general fund salary costs, outreach salary costs, and so on. In practice, every income or expenditure category needs to be clearly labelled with the fund to which it relates.

Provided your books are structured in this way, it is not too difficult to draw out the relevant figures and produce a separate income and expenditure account for each fund, showing what has come in and what has gone out purely on that fund. You may need this for reporting to funders, but it is also vital so that your trustees can monitor each fund separately. Sometimes a charity will find itself relatively well off in cash terms, but if nearly all the money relates to restricted funds, the position on general fund expenditure may be very tight.

Some charities try to avoid proper fund accounting during the year and leave it to an accountant to sort out at year end. But this can be disastrous: you can easily find you have been spending money a fund does not have. At the end of the day, if money given for restricted funds has been spent on other purposes, your trustees will have committed a breach of trust.

One crucial issue for fund accounting is that a restricted fund will generally continue for more than one accounting year: money given for the new roof or the new outreach worker may not be spent until the next year or later. In that case, in your books you need to be able to work out at year end the balance on the restricted fund (i.e. the income for that fund, less the expenses already incurred) and carry it forward as a restricted 'pot' of resources into next year's accounts. This is clearly very different from the situation described at the start of this chapter, for departments of a business, where all the profits would come together at year end.

Most conventional training for bookkeepers assumes that there will be a single brought forward figure for 'reserves' at the start of an accounting year, but clearly in a charity with more than one fund, you need a separate figure for each fund for the balance brought forward at the start of the year. We will look at the implications of this in chapter 5. When producing an income and expenditure account for a fund, it needs to show not just the income and expenditure for the year, but also the balance brought forward on the fund at the start of the year (unless it is a new fund). Similarly, if the project has to continue the following year, you may need the fund to show a substantial balance carried forward at year end, and this needs to be considered when budgeting.

Do we need separate bank accounts?

Many people think fund accounting is easily solved by having a separate bank account for each fund. Sometimes funders seem to imply this, by saying they want their grant held in a separate account, but they usually just mean a separate fund.

However, as you will have seen from the explanation above, provided your books are properly labelled to show the income and expenditure for each fund, and provided you have a separate 'balance forward' for each fund at year end, you don't need separate bank accounts to keep track of different funds. This is the same whether the accounts are on an receipts and payments or an accruals basis.

In some cases a very small organisation with limited bookkeeping skills may find separate bank accounts helpful. But once you get more than a couple of funds it can become totally unmanageable. If you have reasonable sums in hand at any one time you will probably want a deposit account as well as a current account – this means two bank accounts for each fund. Then, if you need petty cash, you will have to apply the same principle and have a separate petty cash tin for each fund.

It can soon get to the point that a charity with just eight funds will have money held in 24 places. Ensuring that cheques are written on the right account becomes a nightmare. If a bill arrives that needs to be split between more than one fund, you will have to write multiple cheques. And once a cheque is inadvertently written from the wrong account, getting everything sorted out is much worse than managing with one bank account in the first place.

Also, you will normally find you can get much more bank interest if you have one high interest deposit account and just keep enough money in a current account for the short term requirements of the charity as a whole. (See chapter 4 for more on managing investment income.)

Similarly, where you need petty cash, one cash tin is fine, so long as all petty cash expenses are clearly marked to show the fund to which they relate (and from a security point of view this is much more manageable).

Transfers between funds

Fund accounting sometimes requires a special transaction in the books – an 'inter-fund transfer'. Clearly this is unique to charity accounting, so you won't find it in normal bookkeeping textbooks.

An inter-fund transfer arises when money or resources need to be transferred from one fund to another. You might feel this goes against the principles of fund accounting, and certainly such transfers cannot be made on a whim, but there are actually several situations where such transfers are needed.

We have already considered the case of transferring money from a general fund to a designated fund (for example a fund for long term repairs) – this is a simple example of an inter-fund transfer. However, sometimes trustees will want to transfer funds from the general fund to a restricted fund where a new project is being partly funded by an external grant, but where the charity is agreeing to support it partly from general funds.

Also, transfers can sometimes be made from a restricted fund to a general fund, if the funder has agreed. For example, the costs of a project may include a 'management fee' to cover the general overheads of the charity in running the project. If it was clearly agreed with the funder that part of the grant would be spent on these management costs, a transfer of the management fee can be made from the restricted fund to the general fund. (An alternative is to split all costs between funds in the first place, but where a management fee relates to general overheads, a funds transfer is usually clearer.)

If the different funds are held in the same bank account, a funds transfer is just a 'paper' entry, but it is, of course, a very important entry, and should only be made if specifically agreed by the trustees. In the books, a funds transfer is, in effect, expenditure from one fund which becomes income to another fund – but of course there is no income or expenditure by the charity as a whole.

The importance of this is shown in the year end accounts, where transfers between funds must appear as a separate line on the SOFA, so they are not confused with external income or expenditure (see figure 7.2).

4 Financial management

Managing the money is central to the work of a charity: it is much more than just a matter of good bookkeeping. In fact, unless you are clear about the sources of your income and how decisions are made about its use, the day to day bookkeeping can be quite meaningless. In a charity, the role of financial management has many features specific to the sector.

Financial responsibility

In a charity, the overall financial responsibility rests with the trustees as a whole. However, in practice, one of the hardest skills for a charity treasurer or finance worker is to enable the trustees to exercise this responsibility effectively so that all major financial decisions are taken by them on an informed basis.

As noted in chapter 2, the trustees have a legal duty to ensure that proper accounting records are kept, but clearly it is impracticable for all trustees to be involved in all the day to day financial transactions of recording receipts, paying bills and salaries, and so on. This must be delegated in some manner – there are several ways of doing this.

It is usual for one of the trustees to be designated as the treasurer of the organisation; within the trustees as a whole he or she will then take particular responsibility for financial issues. Sometimes the term 'honorary treasurer' is used to make it clear that it is a voluntary role. This role can operate in three ways.

- In many small local charities, the treasurer actually does all the bookkeeping, payment of salaries, liaison with the bank and similar tasks. He or she is personally responsible for producing the year end accounts (or for arranging this to be done by the auditor or independent examiner) and often handles much correspondence on financial issues, for example arranging insurance.
- In slightly larger charities, a member of staff may be employed (often part-time) to act as bookkeeper, or there is an administrator whose duties include bookkeeping. The usual arrangement is that the treasurer determines the broad financial procedures and the

categories used in the books (see chapter 5) while the bookkeeper handles the detailed work.

In this case the day to day financial procedures are shared between the treasurer and bookkeeper, for example the treasurer might indicate the type of management report required for the trustees meeting, but the bookkeeper might actually produce it.

- In medium and larger charities, it is impossible for a voluntary treasurer to have any more than a broad overview of the financial arrangements. In such cases the paid managers of the organisation are expected to manage the financial affairs, and simply consult the trustees on major financial decisions. There will usually be a senior member of staff with a job title of finance officer or, in organisations operating on a national scale, finance director.

  In organisations working on this model, the treasurer's role is less formal, as the finance officer would attend trustee meetings and present reports directly. The treasurer will meet from time to time with the finance officer to discuss financial policy, will propose formal resolutions of a financial nature at trustees' meetings, and will liaise with the auditors on issues at trustee level. But usually such treasurers have limited day to day involvement.

The first model has the advantage of simplicity, but as an organisation grows it can become dragged down by too much dependence on a voluntary treasurer. For example, the key member of staff – the manager – may have no financial information if all books are kept at the treasurer's home, and there may be considerable delays in raising cheques.

However, once a paid bookkeeper is appointed, the relationship between the treasurer and bookkeeper is crucial: the bookkeeper needs the direction of the treasurer on financial procedures; equally, the treasurer needs information from the bookkeeper in order to report to the trustees. This all has to be handled with sensitivity, and if there is a paid manager, the treasurer needs to take care not to treat the bookkeeper as one of the treasurer's own staff.

In the third model the relationship of knowledge may well be the other way round: even a treasurer who is a professional in the accounting or banking world is unlikely to have as much knowledge and experience of charity finance as a full time charity finance director. The latter may well be attending conferences on charity finance and meeting with others in organisations such as the Charity Finance Directors Group. Certainly the treasurer will not have the detailed financial knowledge of the organisation concerned. In such cases, the accountant or finance director may have to take on a gentle educational role, appraising the treasurer of major financial issues affecting the charity.

When it works well, this can be a fruitful relationship, especially if the treasurer takes the lead on difficult issues that would otherwise make the finance officer unpopular. The treasurer of a large charity must also take the lead on the issue of proposing the remuneration of senior staff.

However, whatever the size of the charity, it is vital that the treasurer and finance staff accept that they are ultimately the servants of the trustees as a whole. Far too many small charities end up with the treasurer alone deciding what can or cannot be afforded. Finance officers can sometimes make the same mistake. It is the responsibility of treasurers or finance officers to advise the trustees, and to give them sufficient information on which to make an informed decision. But financial decisions, like all decisions, must ultimately be made by the trustees as a whole.

Managing the income and expenditure

Most financial management comes down to decisions about income or expenditure, though, as we saw in the last chapter, where a charity has several funds, you need to look at each fund individually.

In general, you might think the key task would be to maximise the income and minimise the expenditure. But in an organisation where you are not seeking to make a profit it is more complex than this. Of course you want to avoid wasted expenditure – especially as the charity will usually be spending other people's money – but you are not seeking to get the expenditure as low as possible in order to maximise a profit. Most charities have to spend money in order to advance their charitable objects, so cutting down on worthwhile expenditure actually reduces the charity's effectiveness.

However, it is vital to consider both sides of the income and expenditure account. Where a charity is struggling to make ends meet, there are always two choices – to cut the expenses or to increase the income – but often people only consider one or the other. Often the best course is to do some of each.

On the other hand, if the charity (or a certain fund) is doing well and achieving higher income or lower expenses than expected, financial management involves being creative in identifying new areas of expenditure, so that the objects can be further advanced. If you cannot do this, your reserves will just grow (see *Cashflow and reserves*, page 40) perhaps to levels that will bring the charity into criticism. In extreme cases, where income is increasing and there are few ways to spend it, the trustees may need to get the charity's objects changed (in England and Wales this is done by applying to the Charity Commission to make a 'scheme', allowing a charity's funds to be applied to new purposes).

However, on a day to day basis, managing expenditure in a charity is not particularly different to any other organisation – setting sensible budgets and monitoring expenses against them is usually the best approach (see chapter 9 for more on management accounts). But the management of income in a charity can involve several issues unique to this sector.

Fundraising

What a charity can actually do to advance its objects is usually constrained by the income it can generate. It follows that attracting sufficient income is a key role of all charity trustees – this is what is meant by charity fundraising. Curiously, many charities use the term 'fundraising' only to refer to certain types of income generation and some, especially religious charities, object to the word completely. But the term 'fundraising' simply means the process of raising or securing sufficient funds to support the work of the charity. So whether you are asking for committed gifts, applying for grants, selling goods or services or maximising investment income, fundraising is all about raising the resources to support the charity's aims.

Some charities will have another trustee who co-ordinates the fundraising, quite separate from the treasurer, and where staff are employed there may be a paid fundraiser separate from the finance officer. But treasurers and finance officers need to understand the financial implications of different sources of income. (The links between accounting and fundraising are considered further in chapter 12.)

Sources of income

Fundamentally, there are three main ways in which a charity can get income:

- donations;
- trading;
- investment.

Donated income

Any money given to a charity counts as donated income. As explained in earlier chapters, this ability to attract gifts – often for nothing in return – is at the heart of what it means to be a charity.

Donated income includes any of the following:

- coins placed in a collecting tin or collecting plate;
- a gift from an individual by cheque or standing order;
- a gift from an individual deducted through their payroll;
- a grant or donation from a charitable trust or lottery distributor;
- a grant or donation from a company (provided they are not seeking anything in return);
- a grant from a local authority or public sector funder (provided it is genuinely a grant – see below);
- a legacy to the charity in someone's will.

In the case of individual donations to charity, there are very attractive tax rules for direct gifts, payroll gifts and legacies, and with proper understanding of these, a charity can often increase the value of donations considerably (see chapter 12). Some charities make extensive use of Gift Aid, for example, but many others are missing out.

Some grants and donations will be for unrestricted funds; others will be tied to specific projects or activities, and thus need to be allocated to restricted funds (or occasionally to a capital fund if it was a capital appeal (see chapter 3 for an explanation of these terms).

When money is *given* to a charity the relationship is one of trust. If the money is misused, the trustees could be guilty of a breach of trust and might have to reimburse the funder. But there is no contractual relationship. Even if you have a public sector funder that makes a grant with ten pages of conditions on how it is to be used, it is still a grant to a (very) restricted fund. The funder isn't purchasing anything from the charity (if they want that, they will need a contract – see below).

Some funders like to describe their funding agreements as *service level agreements* (SLAs). You sometimes need to read the small print to work out whether an SLA is actually a grant or a contract, but most are in fact grants (restricted not just in terms of purpose, but restricted also to a certain service level that must be achieved).

Trading income

The second main source of income is trading income – charging for goods or services. When charities get income in this way they are working more like ordinary businesses, but there are still many differences.

Many people think there is some rule preventing charities from trading, but although there are certain limits and tax implications (see chapter 11) trading income is a normal source of income in many charities.

Trading income can include any of the following:

- an educational charity charging fees for places on courses;
- a housing charity charging rents to tenants;
- a charity selling books or publications (where the content was related to the charity's objects);
- a religious charity charging fees for weddings or funerals;
- a counselling charity charging fees for counselling sessions (where a definite charge is made, rather than just asking for a donation);
- a membership charity charging membership fees (where the member gets a definite benefit under the charity's objects – if there is no benefit, the member's subscription is just a donation);
- a health or disability charity charging fees under a contract with the public sector for providing services to people with certain medical conditions.

These would all be referred to as *primary purpose trading* – because what the charity is supplying is directly related to its objects.

For some charities, primary purpose trading is the main source of income. If a funder wants your charity to do work under a contract (rather than a grant) this is a contractual relationship, and the income is trading income. The funder has become a customer, purchasing services, and if the charity fails to deliver the services properly, it could be liable for breach of contract. So before entering into major contracts, charities should normally seek legal advice.

Trading income also includes:

- selling tickets for a fundraising event;
- selling mugs, tee-shirts, cards or souvenirs to raise money;
- selling raffle tickets (this is not a pure donation, because the purchaser may win a prize);
- providing advertising or sponsorship opportunities to companies (where they gain substantial publicity);
- selling second-hand goods in a charity shop or jumble sale;
- selling the charity's services in a way that is outside its objects: for example providing places on courses to people who are outside the charity's beneficiaries, or renting out rooms to commercial organisations.

These are classed as *trading for fundraising purposes* – because what you are supplying is not part of the charity's objects; the reason for the activity is simply to raise funds. In deciding whether an activity is raising donations, or whether it is trading for fundraising purposes, the key issue to ask is: 'Does the supporter get any significant benefit?'

There are few restrictions on primary purpose trading by charities, although VAT sometimes has to be considered. But there are strict limits on trading for fundraising purposes, and above these limits the charity could be liable to tax (see chapter 11). Activities such as selling raffle (lottery) tickets or selling alcohol also have other legal controls.

In terms of the accounts, primary purpose trading income will normally be posted to unrestricted funds. This can sometimes make a contract more attractive than a grant. You may wish to use a designated fund to keep track of a certain contract-funded project, but the charity's obligation is simply to supply the goods or services contracted: if you are able to do this at less than the price agreed, any profit or surplus can be retained by the charity to support the development of services. This is quite different from the trust relationship that applies with grants, where unspent funds may have to be returned. (If you have funders who object to this, and want you to treat their contract as a restricted fund with any surplus being returned to them, ask whether they expect that arrangement with other purchases – for example their stationery suppliers.)

Whilst a surplus on trading income may be attractive, remember that if you have under-costed the work and cannot negotiate an increase in the fee, the charity may still be legally obliged to carry out the work, and you may end up subsidising it from other unrestricted income.

Trading income for fundraising purposes will also usually go to unrestricted funds, unless you specifically asked people to buy tickets or support an event on the basis that the proceeds would be used to support a certain project.

Investment income

Investment income includes any of the following:

- bank interest;
- dividends on shares;
- rents on investment properties (where a charity specifically holds property for investment purposes – very rare in small charities).

For many local charities the only investment income will be small amounts of bank interest. But for some charities where there are substantial endowments, investments may be the main source of income; this is the case for many grant-making trusts.

Charities are entitled to a number of tax concessions on investment income: for example interest can be paid gross (you simply need to provide evidence to your bank that the organisation is a charity), and there is no capital gains tax to pay when investments increase in value. Until recently, charities could reclaim advance corporation tax on share dividends, but since 1997 this has been gradually phased out.

Investment income should normally be allocated to the fund to which the investments belong. In theory, this means that where several funds are held in the same bank account, the bank interest should be split between the different funds on a reasonable basis. However, with normal restricted projects where the funder expects that the money will be spent fairly soon after receipt, few funders will be that prescriptive, and many charities are thus able to allocate all bank interest to the general fund. But if you have a long term appeal such as a building fund, where substantial amounts are raised perhaps a year or more before they can be spent, donors have a right to expect that interest on their donations will be added to the fund concerned.

However, with a capital (endowment) fund, the terms of the endowment will normally require that income is allocated to some other fund. (If the income just went back into the endowment fund, it would just keep growing and would never be spent on the charity's objects – accounting in this way has prompted Charity Commission investigations.) But with shares and similar investments, take care to distinguish the investment income (dividends etc.) from capital growth – the latter will remain in the capital fund unless the charity has formal approval for other approaches.

Managing different forms of income

As explained, the trustees have a duty to maximise the income of the charity in order to further the objects and the treasurer or finance officer will usually play a part in implementing this.

With *donated income* the key issue is an effective fundraising strategy. Some charities just accept donations passively, but if the work of your charity is worthwhile, you have an obligation to ask people to support it. With grant income, the charity usually needs to be pro-active in applying for grants, and planning well ahead where grant income has a finite life.

With *primary purpose trading* the key issue is usually how to price the goods or services you are supplying, and then how to market that service. Since the trade is seeking to advance the charity's objects, you will usually be aiming to break even rather than to make a profit on the activity: generally keeping the price down will enable you to reach more people. But, unlike business trading, remember that with a charity the customer (the funder) is often quite different from the client or beneficiary who will be using your service. However, if you are offering something that will be paid for directly by your beneficiaries, you may deliberately want to price the service below the cost price, using other income to subsidise the service.

With *trading for fundraising purposes*, again pricing and marketing are key issues, but this time the aim is usually to set the price as high as possible (but without actually putting people off). There is no point in running a fundraising activity that simply breaks even. If people are giving voluntary time to help run an event, the charity needs to make a substantial return to justify their time and effort.

Management of *investment income* is sometimes just a case of choosing the best deposit account, but for charities with large funds to manage, the management of investments may take up a good part of the time at trustees' meetings. Since the Trustee Act 2000, trustees have much more flexibility in managing investments, but where significant sums are involved they have an obligation to seek professional advice. In such cases, you need to determine an investment policy, which must be stated in the charity's annual report (see chapter 7).

Managing core costs

Much of the financial management will deal with each fund individually; as explained you cannot use income to a restricted fund to subsidise deficits elsewhere.

But the relative outcome of each fund is often determined by how overheads (such as the running costs of the charity's premises) are apportioned between funds, or how much you can negotiate in management fees in order to permit transfers from restricted to unrestricted funds.

It is vital to appreciate that when taking on a new project (for example, involving a new worker) the costs are much more than that person's salary costs and direct project expenses. For example:

- the new person will take up some of the manager's time in supervision;
- he or she will occupy part of your premises (even if the premises are already there, the running costs will usually increase);
- the new worker may need to use the charity's existing equipment (computers, photocopier, possibly vehicles), giving higher maintenance costs;
- the new project will generate additional transactions in your accounts, which may require extra hours for your bookkeeper;
- the extra complexity of the charity's affairs may require additional trustees' meetings;
- the extra income may take the charity over a threshold for its final accounts (see chapter 2);
- if the project finishes and you cannot offer the person other work, you may have to meet redundancy costs;
- the process of bidding for the funds in the first place may have taken up the time of a co-ordinator or fundraiser.

Different funders have different policies on meeting such costs, and as treasurer or finance officer you need to be aware of these. Some charities find they can *only* secure project funding, and unless you can agree reasonable management fees with your funders, you may find you have no unrestricted funds at all. Some funders dislike the term 'management fee', but are nevertheless willing to pay for a proportion of a manager's time in other ways.

However, taking on new projects without sufficient support for core costs can actually be a drain on other resources of the charity. Sometimes trustees will agree it is worth taking on a new project, knowing that it will need subsidising, because it is sufficiently worthwhile in terms of the charity's objects. But sometimes your task may be to advise the trustees to decline a new project, even if it seems attractive in other ways, if the core costs will not be sufficiently covered.

Cashflow and reserves

In any organisation, it is not enough just to balance the income and expenditure, it is also necessary to ensure that there is sufficient money in hand at any one time to meet immediate expenses. Otherwise a charity, like any other organisation, can become insolvent.

Given the uncertainty of much charity income, this management of cashflow often requires more care than in other organisations.

In practice, the difficulties are greatest with trading income, and with charities whose donated income is subject to major seasonal fluctuations (for example Christmas appeals). In most cases, donated income can be received before the money has to be spent. Grants are often paid quarterly or half-yearly in advance (although problems can be acute if a grant is late – some public sector funders are well-known for this).

However, trading income often requires expenditure on salaries or materials before the work can be invoiced, and then there may be a delay of a month or more awaiting payment of the charity's invoice. It is vital to plan for this – see chapter 9 on preparing a cashflow forecast.

Issues of cashflow lead naturally to considering the appropriate level of reserves a charity should have – the amount available in general unrestricted funds. (If you are doing accruals accounting, and if the balance of your general fund includes fixed assets, you need to deduct these from the fund balance to get the reserves figure.)

The Charity Commission has had to remind charities from time to time that accumulating money is not itself a charitable purpose. Generally, a charity is expected to spend its income on advancing its objects, unless there is a specific reason for keeping it. There is no problem in retaining money if there is a clear development plan, for example to acquire a new building in a few years' time. But retaining large amounts towards general running costs is not acceptable, this is seen as putting the needs of future (unknown) beneficiaries ahead of current (known) beneficiaries.

There is also a problem that some grant-makers will refuse to help charities with significant reserves – but this can encourage inappropriate expenditure prior to year end, just to bring the reserves down to a more acceptable level.

Different charities will need different levels of reserves: a small grant making charity which only makes one-off grants (i.e. no long term obligations) may be able to manage with almost no reserves. On the other hand, a service-providing charity running a number of complex projects with uncertain income streams will usually need running costs amounting to at least three months' average expenditure. Where the income is very seasonal, or where long term commitments are made (for example in a charity funding medical research) much higher reserves may be needed.

The Charity Commission strongly encourages all charities to set a specific reserves policy, and where a policy has been agreed it must be stated in the charity's annual report.

Where the reserves are unacceptably low, it may for a few years be necessary to budget for general fund income to be more than expenditure, until reserves have reached a sensible level. Conversely, some charities have realised over the years that their reserves have become unnecessarily high, and are now spending them by increasing their activities.

5 Bookkeeping principles

Some people think that bookkeeping is the heart of a treasurer's work and might be surprised to see just one chapter devoted to this. But bookkeeping cannot be done in isolation, you need an appreciation of the issues discussed in the earlier chapters in order to decide where in the books to allocate particular transactions. You also need to consider what will be needed for management accounts (see chapter 9) and final accounts (chapter 7) in order to decide what categories to use in your books.

Who does what?

Effective bookkeeping depends just as much on the human interactions in the process as on the books themselves. Once the charity reaches the size where day to day bookkeeping is done by a member of staff, rather than by the treasurer personally, communication between the treasurer, bookkeeper and manager is vital to the task (see chapter 4).

Bookkeeping is not just a mechanical exercise: decisions have to be made about what to post where; sometimes a cost has to be apportioned between more than one fund; you need to know if some incoming money is actually a debtor from last year; and so on. Also, new categories and even new funds will need to be added to the books from time to time, such as when the charity receives a grant or donation for a new purpose.

So employing a bookkeeper for just half a day a week, for example, is often not very successful. Often such bookkeepers never really gain sufficient knowledge of the charity to make informed decisions, so they either make assumptions (which often have to be corrected at year end, involving a lot of extra time and cost) or, to do the job properly, they have to ask so many questions that you feel it would quicker to keep the books yourself. The same problem arises with treasurers who are frequently absent from trustees' meetings.

Also, bear in mind that much treasurers' and bookkeepers' time is taken up with paying bills, banking receipts, chasing outstanding payments and a whole host of related issues. Actually 'posting' (putting) entries in the books rarely accounts for more than perhaps a quarter of the total time.

In practice, operating any bookkeeping system, whether manual or computerised, can be split into three levels:

1 Devising the basic structure of the accounts – drawing up the layout and allocating columns with manual books, or defining a chart of accounts (the list of account headings) in a computer system.

2 Posting entries in the books on a day to day basis (together with day to day checks such as bank reconciliation – see chapter 6).

3 Closing off the books at the end of an accounting period, working out total figures for each category, and transferring these into appropriate reports for use by others. A very small charity can do this just once a year, but larger charities will usually want monthly or quarterly accounting periods.

Where roles are separated between a treasurer and bookkeeper, the treasurer needs to be involved in levels 1 and 3, but level 2 is usually handled by the bookkeeper alone, except where problems and queries arise. However, an experienced finance officer may handle all three levels, only consulting the treasurer where policy decisions are required.

The format of the books

Clearly any bookkeeping system must keep a record of all financial transactions affecting the charity. Without a list of individual receipts and payments it is impossible to establish monthly or yearly figures with any certainty.

The simple cashbook

The simplest form of books is just a list of transactions, usually split into columns for receipts and payments.

Date	Cheque no	Details	Receipts	Payments
3 Jan	000271	Rent		250.00
21 Feb	000272	Wages to administrator		83.33
27 Feb	Paid in	Grant from council	2,000.00	
12 Mar	000273	Jones & Co – printing		78.00
19 Mar	Paid in	Cash – proceeds of concert	43.90	
21 Mar	000274	Wages to administrator		83.33

Certainly this format keeps a record of transactions. However, it is worth noting that with systems of this kind, what you write in the 'details' or 'comment' column is vital in order to know at a later date what the transaction was about. A slight improvement, to ensure you know why each transaction was entered, is to have two narrative columns – one for the name of the payee or funder and one explaining the purpose or reason for the receipt or payment.

Date	Cheque no	Payee/donor	Purpose	Receipts	Payments
3 Jan	000271	ABC Properties	Rent		250.00
21 Feb	000272	R Jones	Admin wages		83.33
27 Feb	Paid in	Midsham Council	Annual grant	2,000.00	
12 Mar	000273	Jones & Co	Printing		78.00
19 Mar	Paid in	Cash	Concert proceeds	43.90	
21 Mar	000274	R Jones	Admin wages		83.33

You can draw up a layout of this kind on any kind of book or plain paper, although you will find stationery shops sell a wide range of books already set out in suitable columns. A book has the advantage over separate sheets in that pages are unlikely to get lost, and there is less risk of fraud from someone taking out pages and changing them.

But although this provides a record of transactions, it cannot be said to be a full bookkeeping system, until we look at the issue of 'closing off' the books, and adding in whatever funds were in hand at the start of the accounting period.

There are various ways of 'balancing off' books at the end of a period. In general, you will want to total the payments and receipts and subtract the payments from the receipts to determine the surplus for the period. You then need to add on the funds in hand at the start of the period, in order to know the balance in hand to carry forward to the next period.

Date	Cheque no	Payee/donor	Purpose	Receipts	Payments
31 Dec	Balance carried forward			373.45	
3 Jan	000271	ABC Properties	Rent		250.00
21 Feb	000272	R Jones	Admin wages		83.33
27 Feb	Paid in	Midsham Council	Annual grant	2,000.00	
12 Mar	000273	Jones & Co	Printing		678.00
19 Mar	Paid in	Cash	Concert proceeds	43.90	
21 Mar	000274	R Jones	Admin wages		83.33
31 Mar	Totals for quarter			2,043.90	1,094.66
	Subtract payments			-1,094.66	
	Net surplus for quarter (receipts less payments)			949.24	
	Add on balance brought forward at 31 Dec			373.45	
31 Mar	Balance carried forward			1,322.69	

Now that the books have been totalled and closed off, from this simple cashbook you have the figures to produce some helpful management accounts for the quarter for the trustees.

Books like this are quite adequate for a very small charity where everything is done through one bank account and where there are no more than perhaps 30 or so transactions per year. But if you had several hundred transactions, this format would be quite limiting because it doesn't show in any overall manner where the income and expenditure has come from. Going through a list of more than 100 entries, looking at the purpose of each in order to produce sensible year end accounts, would be a great deal of work.

Analysed cashbook (single fund)

An easy but very useful improvement on the simple cashbook is an analysed cashbook. Rather than just having single columns for 'receipts' and 'payments' you have a number of columns into which the income and expenditure is analysed. Whenever you post an entry, you take care to write it in the correct column. Most manual bookkeeping systems are based on the use of one or more analysed cashbooks.

Date	Cheque No	Payee/Donor	Purpose	Balance Forward	Receipts		Payments		
					Grants	Fund-raising	Premises	Wages	Print/ stationery
31 Dec	Balance carried forward			373.45					
3 Jan	000271	ABC Properties	Rent				250.00		
21 Feb	000272	R Jones	Admin wages					83.33	
27 Feb	Paid in	Midsham Council	Annual grant		2,000.00				
12 Mar	000273	Jones & Co	Printing						678.00
19 Mar	Paid in	Cash	Concert			43.90			
21 Mar	000274	R Jones	Admin wages					83.33	
31 Mar	Totals for quarter for each category			373.45	2,000.00	43.90	250.00	166.66	678.00
	Total receipts and payments					2,043.90			1,094.66
	Subtract payments from receipts					–1,096.66			
	Net surplus for quarter			949.24		949.24			
31 Mar	Balance carried forward			1,322.69					

However, even with just two columns of receipts and three columns of payments it is difficult to show them on a single page, and in reality most charities will need many more categories of income and expenditure. Some people combine the 'Balance forward' column with another column, but it is clearer if you can keep it separate.

The best way of creating more space is to keep two separate cashbooks, one for receipts and one for payments – see pages 48–49. Both the receipts and payments must, of course, be closed off at the same date.

It is possible to buy books with around 16 columns across a double page spread. Some columns will be used for dates, descriptions and cheque numbers, so it is usually possible to have up to about 12 categories of analysis. With separate books for receipts and payments, this will give you around 12 income categories and 12 expenditure categories.

However, one advantage of the simple cashbook and analysed cashbooks above is that it is quite easy, if you wish, to add an extra column for the running bank balance (in the second example, you could use the balance forward column). Once you keep receipts and payments on separate pages, you will find this more difficult. But it is not necessarily a problem if you can keep the bank balance somewhere else, such as a running balance on cheque stubs.

Analysed cashbook (multiple funds)

However, in many charities the bookkeeping must distinguish several funds. This means considerably more columns because, as explained in chapter 3, you must be able to distinguish receipts and payments for each fund. However, if you have no more than two or three funds, and if you don't need too many categories for each, you can still work with two analysed cashbooks – one for receipts and one for payments.

In such cases, remember that you need a separate balance forward for *each* fund – this is usually shown in the receipts book.

RECEIPTS BOOK

Date	Receipt Ref	From	Purpose	GENERAL FUND				OUTREACH FUND		
				Balance forward	Grants	Fund-raising	Interest	Balance forward	Grants	Participation fees
31 Dec	Balances carried forward			373.45				0.00		
14 Jan	Deposit	Midsham Trust	Outreach grant						800.00	
27 Feb	DC	Midsham Council	General grant		2,000.00					
3 Mar	Deposit	Cash	Concert			43.90				
19 Mar	Deposit	Cash	Outing							24.00
30 Mar	Int	Midwest Bank	Interest Jan–Mar				3.27			
31 Mar	Totals for quarter for each category			373.45	2,000.00	43.90	3.27	0.00	800.00	24.00
	Total receipts for each fund						2,047.17			824.00
	Subtract payments (from PAYMENTS book)						–1,109.66			–591.21
	Net surplus for quarter for each fund			937.51			937.51	232.79		232.79
31 Mar	Balances carried forward			1,310.96				232.79		

PAYMENTS BOOK

Date	Cheque No	Payee	Purpose	GENERAL FUND				OUTREACH FUND		
				Premises	Wages	Print/ stationery	Trustees	Wages	Travel	Activities
3 Jan	000271	ABC Properties	Rent	250.00						
21 Feb	000272	R Jones	Admin wages		83.33					
21 Feb	000273	J Smiley	Outreach wages					230.00		
27 Feb	000274	K Patel	Travel expenses				15.00			
3 Mar	000275	K Patel	Outreach travel						49.84	
12 Mar	000276	Jones & Co	Printing x 2			678.00				52.00
17 Mar	DD	ABC Hire	Play eqt hire							29.37
21 Mar	000277	R Jones	Admin wages		83.33					
21 Mar	000278	J Smiley	Outreach wages					230.00		
31 Mar	Totals for quarter for each category			250.00	166.66	678.00	15.00	460.00	49.84	81.37
	Total payments for each fund						1,109.66			591.21
1 Apr	*(Start of payments for next quarter)*									

Cashbooks for each fund

If you have more than two or three funds, or if you find you need the whole page width to cover all the categories for just one fund, the only solution is to keep separate books for each fund.

Many charities do this, but great care is needed with a transaction that is split across funds. In the example on page 49, the printers Jones & Co have clearly invoiced two printing jobs together – one relating to the General Fund and the other to Outreach – and a single cheque number 000276 has been written for £730 to cover this. But the cost is actually split into separate columns: £678 to 'General fund printing and stationery' and £52 to 'Outreach activities'. On a single page, it is fairly easy to read across the line, but with separate books, extensive cross referencing is needed in such cases.

This shows the limits of single entry bookkeeping, and if you have split transactions arising regularly, double entry bookkeeping (see page 52) is to be recommended.

Multiple bank accounts and petty cash

The examples above assume that all receipts and payments go into a single bank account. This certainly keeps things simple, because your books do not need to show where a receipt is paid into, or which account a cheque is written on. If you can bank all receipts as soon as they arrive and make all payments by cheque, it is much easier than keeping temporary amounts in petty cash.

Deposit accounts

Many charities will need a deposit account of some kind, but provided this is only used for transfers to and from the current account, it doesn't add any great complication. Normal receipts and payments will go via the current account, so the main cashbook is unaffected.

It is helpful to keep a separate note of the running balance of the deposit account, with details of transfers in and out (just as you will, hopefully, keep a running balance on the current account in the cheque book). But if you are keeping accounts broken down by fund (as required for charities – rather than broken down by bank account) transfers to or from the deposit account do not appear in the payments or receipts. You are simply transferring the assets of the charity from one account to another, but the charity hasn't actually received any new funds or paid anything out.

When you get interest on the deposit account, you need to post this in the books as a receipt, and it is easiest if the bank will agree to pay deposit account interest into the current account. If not, remember that deposit account interest needs recording both in the receipts book *and* in your record of deposit account movements.

Handling multiple cheque accounts and petty cash

If you sometimes pay large cheques directly into the deposit account, or if you have more than one account on which cheques can be written, your books need to be more elaborate. This is also the case if you keep money in, and sometimes make payments directly from, petty cash.

The best way to treat petty cash is just like another bank account. So when you draw money from the bank for petty cash, remember that no money is going out of the charity even though you are writing a cheque: it is just like transferring assets between current and deposit accounts. It is only when you spend petty cash that you actually have payments to enter in the payments book.

Some people make the mistake of just adding an extra column to the payments book for 'Petty cash drawn', but of course this does not explain the purpose of the expenditure and, in any case, not all the petty cash drawn will necessarily be spent. At year end, if all the petty cash expenses have been lumped into one column, a lot of work is needed to go through petty cash books and break down the expenditure: it is much better to do this during the year as petty cash is spent. Also, with a bank account, you can rely on the bank to keep certain records, but with petty cash it is all down to you. So, as well as your normal books, it is vital to have a system of petty cash vouchers or a petty cash book where cash expenses are immediately noted. From time to time (perhaps once a month) you can transfer the total petty cash expenses into the main payments book, split into columns as required.

If you take in cash receipts (for example from collections, events or charity shops) it is usually best to bank the receipts gross, and deal with petty cash expenses separately. If you start reimbursing expenses out of cash received it needs very thorough bookkeeping to keep track of what is happening and to satisfy your auditor or examiner.

Many people think petty cash accounting is simple, but in fact it makes life a lot more complicated. It needs considerably more skills to keep accounts correctly in an organisation where petty cash is widely used. It is much easier if small expenses can be met personally by staff or trustees and then reimbursed promptly by cheque. Provided you devise a proper expense claim form for such cases, this is much easier to trace.

To handle receipts and payments made directly from petty cash or from an alternative bank account, you need an extra column in your payments and receipts books to show which account has been used in each case. But it then becomes much harder to reconcile your receipts and payments to your bank accounts. To be sure your figures are correct, you really need to keep a running balance for each bank and petty cash account.

Once you do this, you are effectively posting every transaction into two places in your books (or 'ledgers' as they are sometimes called) – to the receipts or payments ledger and to the bank or petty cash ledger (you need a separate bank/petty cash ledger for each bank account and each pot of petty cash). This is called *double entry bookkeeping*.

Double entry bookkeeping

The bookkeeping systems shown in the previous illustrations are all single entry systems, where each amount is written in one place only. But professional bookkeepers will normally use double entry bookkeeping, where everything is written in two places.

Double entry bookkeeping is more work, but it has the advantage that it can cope even with very complex systems, and its internal checks help to detect errors. Even if you have seven bank accounts, three petty cash accounts, 15 funds with 40 or more income and expenditure categories in each fund, reliable manual books can be kept on a double entry basis.

The concept of double entry bookkeeping relies on having a number of ledgers, with just two columns in each, called 'debits' and 'credits'. So rather than trying to have vast numbers of columns across the page, you keep each account as a separate ledger. These can be done in a book with just two columns per page (plus space for dates and comments) and a separate page for each ledger. (Note that with fund accounting, you cannot have just one ledger for a fund: you need a separate ledger for each income category and each expenditure category of the fund.)

Any transaction always involves at least two postings: a debit to one account and a credit to another account. (In a split case, you could have two or more credits adding up to a single debit or vice versa, but the debits and credits must always balance.)

Here are some simple examples of double entry transactions:

- £2,000 General fund grant received and paid into bank
  - Debit: Bank £2,000
  - Credit: General Fund grant income £2,000
- £730 Printing bill paid (split between two funds)
  - Credit: Bank £730
  - Debit: General Fund printing/stationery £678
    Debit: Outreach Fund activities £52
- £150 Petty cash drawn (cheque written for cash)
  - Credit: Bank £150
  - Debit: Petty cash £150

People sometimes query why you debit the bank when receiving money, and credit it when paying out: this is the opposite to what you see on bank statements. But the whole concept of debits and credits relates to the notion of debtors and creditors, and if two people enter into a transaction, one person's debtor is another person's creditor. Banks generally produce statements in terms of *their* books – not yours.

So if you deposit money at the bank, from the bank's point of view it is not their money – it is money they owe to you – so in their books it is a creditor, and they show the entry as a credit. But in your books, the bank has money which belongs to you – to you the bank is a debtor. In your books, paying money into the bank is increasing the bank's debts to you, so you post it as a debit. (Think about it in a dark room for a few minutes!)

The same applies with normal commercial transactions: if A sells something to B on an invoice (which is not yet paid), the amount due is a debtor in A's books, but in B's books the amount payable is a creditor. (This is taking us into accruals accounting – see chapter 10. But even with receipts and payments accounting, double entry bookkeeping is very useful if you have several funds or several bank accounts.)

Any double entry system allows you to do a very useful check called a *trial balance*. This means adding up the net balance on every ledger (debits less credits or vice versa) and putting them down as a list. Because the debits and credits have to balance for every transaction, it follows that total debits and total credits should be the same across all the accounts. If you find they aren't, you must have misposted a double entry somewhere.

To run a proper double entry system manually, you can in principle post everything directly to the two ledgers concerned. But because of the risk of posting one half of a double entry and then getting distracted before you have done the second half, it is often best to write everything first of all in a simple cashbook, and then post from there into the ledgers.

In a book of this length there is no space to explain all the details of double entry bookkeeping, but nowadays very few charities (or businesses) do full double entry bookkeeping on a manual basis. Most computer-based accounting systems work internally on a double entry basis (with the guarantee that the debits and credits balance) and at year end your auditor or examiner may ask you to post adjustments in your accounts, which they will usually give you as a list of debits and credits. So whilst few treasurers and administrators are experts in double entry bookkeeping, it is useful to have a general appreciation of how it works.

Manual books or computers?

Although it is quite possible to keep even quite complex books on a manual basis, nowadays most charities start to consider computerising their accounts once there are too many categories for an analysed cashbook. Access to computers is rarely a problem today, and the costs of systems can be very reasonable.

There are three levels of using computers in charity accounting:

- spreadsheets;
- general purpose accounting systems;
- charity-specific accounting systems.

Spreadsheets

A spreadsheet, such as Microsoft Excel or Corel Quattro Pro, allows you to maintain complex financial data in rows and columns, within 'cells'. It can provide more columns than you can get across the page of a normal cashbook, and can total the columns for you automatically. You might therefore feel that a spreadsheet would be better for bookkeeping than manual books.

But spreadsheets have some serious disadvantages if you are trying to set up a complete bookkeeping system. When you open a spreadsheet you have access to all the cells at once, and even in a modest charity with (say) 50 income and expenditure categories (over a number of funds) and 500 transactions per year, your spreadsheet will have 25,000 cells. The size makes it cumbersome, and hard to manage, with a great risk of putting entries in the wrong cell. Moreover, unlike manual books – where corrections are easily spotted if you write the books in ink – there is nothing in a spreadsheet to stop someone changing something entered earlier in the year, so it is easy to wipe out earlier entries that have been checked and balanced.

If you are an expert spreadsheet user some of these issues can be overcome, but this may almost mean writing your own accounting system in spreadsheet macros. Few people therefore rely on spreadsheets as their sole means of bookkeeping, and those who attempt it usually end up keeping extensive manual books as well.

The real value of spreadsheets is for financial analysis, management accounts, budgeting for new projects and the like. They can also allow you to take figures from your accounts and present them in attractive graphical ways.

General purpose accounting systems

If you wish to keep reliable books of account, an accounting system is much better than a spreadsheet. Computer-based accounting systems allow you to define the individual accounts (or ledgers) into which you want your accounts broken down, and then allow you to post transactions using simple methods of input. Because of this, they can maintain an *audit trail* – a list of transactions and where they were allocated – and most such systems use double entry bookkeeping (although, except for unusual transactions, you do not usually have to know about debits and credits).

The audit trail means it is possible to trace with certainty how the final figures are reached. Moreover, you can be certain when posting an entry that it will only affect the accounts intended. You can usually have as many accounts as you wish (or if there is a limit it is very large) – you are not limited to the columns on a page.

Accounting systems do not necessarily save time in terms of recording transactions in the first place: it takes about as long to enter a transaction in a computer-based accounting system as it does to write it in a book. But the big benefit of computer-based accounting systems is that they will produce a wide range of reports automatically from the transactions entered. You can usually print a profit and loss account or balance sheet within a few seconds, and you can do this at any time – whereas with manual books it is very difficult to produce reports except when the books are periodically balanced off.

Of course, any computer system needs time to learn, and care is needed in setting up a sensible chart of accounts in the first place (you may need training to help with this). There is also the risk that if your computer fails, you could lose the whole year's accounts, so it is vital to take regular backups of the files. But actually this is a big advantage of computer systems, because the data can quickly and easily be copied to backup disks when needed, and these can then be taken off site so you could still recover even in the event of a fire or flood. With manual books, to make an off site backup you would have to photocopy every page.

Compared with manual books, computer-based accounting systems thus offer several advantages:

- much better financial information and reports available at any time;
- ability to handle many more categories than are (easily) possible with manual books;
- a huge time saving at end of quarter and end of year;
- a reliable audit trail (no risk of imbalanced double entries, for example);
- much easier to make security backups.

Charity-specific accounting systems

Most general purpose accounting systems are based around the idea of small business accounts (or sometimes domestic household accounts). So although they will keep your transactions and post them to ledgers, it may take a lot of work at year end to get the accounts into the form you need, and you may need help from a professional accountant. In practice, most charities using general purpose accounting systems rely heavily on downloading information into spreadsheets, and then using some spreadsheet manipulations to get what they need. This needs a lot of skill both with the accounting system and the spreadsheet.

One of the main problems is usually fund accounting. As explained in chapter 3, this is quite different from departments within a business, because you need a separate balance forward on each fund. It is vital that you can determine the balance of any fund at any time without a lot of work. Also, at year end you will probably need to produce a statement of financial activities (the SOFA – see chapter 7); if the structure of your accounts is directly linked to this, the process is much easier.

With larger and more complex general purpose accounting systems, it may be possible to define your own reports, but this needs a lot of setting up and you will probably need a fairly sophisticated product with multi-company facilities to do true fund accounting.

However, there are a number of accounting systems designed specifically for use by charities (different products being aimed at different sized organisations). The examples in this book use the *Kubernesis Accounting System*, in whose development the author has been closely involved. A charity-specific accounting system will have fund accounting as a central feature, and may well be able to produce reports such as the SOFA automatically, which greatly simplifies the task of preparing the year-end reports. Also, in the event of problems and queries you are likely to be dealing with a supplier who understands charity accounting and the requirements of the SORP, and the documentation will be designed specifically for charities.

Posting interest, direct debits and similar items

Any bookkeeping system, whether manual or computerised, must show all financial transactions – including those that happen automatically.

There may be some transactions that you do not know about until you get a bank statement; if so don't close off your books until you get the statement that goes to the end of the accounting period.

These entries will not have cheque numbers to show the books, so use codes such as 'DD' (direct debit), 'DC' (direct credit), 'Auto' (automatic payment), 'Int' (interest), 'SO' (standing order) and so on, to make the entry clear.

Bank interest is posted in the books as a normal receipt. Direct debits need entering as normal payments (remember that although a direct debit is a debit in the bank's books, with double entry bookkeeping it will be a credit in your books). If you have incoming standing orders – perhaps for regular donations – enter them as receipts, though if you have a separate computer system for fundraising records it is usually best to enter incoming standing orders first in the fundraising system, and then just transfer a weekly or monthly total into the main accounts.

Posting wages and salaries

For many treasurers, the normal entry of receipts and payments is not too difficult, but wages and salaries can present particular problems because of the rules on tax, national insurance (NI) and other deductions.

Of course, you cannot post salary payments in your accounts until the basic PAYE (Pay As You Earn) calculations have been done. The tasks of a treasurer or finance officer may well include operating a PAYE system for the charity. However, PAYE is not particularly charity-specific: apart from the importance of understanding the distinctions between staff and volunteers, PAYE principles are the same for any organisation employing staff. Plenty of guidance is available both from books (see the *Further reading*) and from your local Inland Revenue office.

PAYE calculations have to be done each time wages or salaries are paid. They can be done manually (using the forms provided by the Inland Revenue) or computerised (if you have a number of staff) or contracted out. Many local charities use the services of an umbrella body such as a local council for voluntary service or a diocesan office to run their PAYE calculations.

Once the PAYE calculations are done, there are generally two payments to make – a net payment to the employee and a payment of taxes and NI to the Inland Revenue (Collector of Taxes). But the numbers can be quite confusing: because there are three separate taxes – the employee's income tax (deducted from his/her salary), the *employee's* NI (also deducted from the salary), and the *employer's* NI, which has to be paid by all employers (including charities) on top of the gross salary due to the employee.

The diagram below shows a possible case (with hypothetical numbers). The employee has earned £1,000 salary this month, from which you must deduct tax (£200 in this case) and employee's NI (£80). So the actually salary cheque – or the amount paid by bank transfer if used – is £720. You must pay these deductions to the Collector of Taxes, together with the £100 of employer's NI on top of the salary. So the total payment to the Collector in this example is £380.

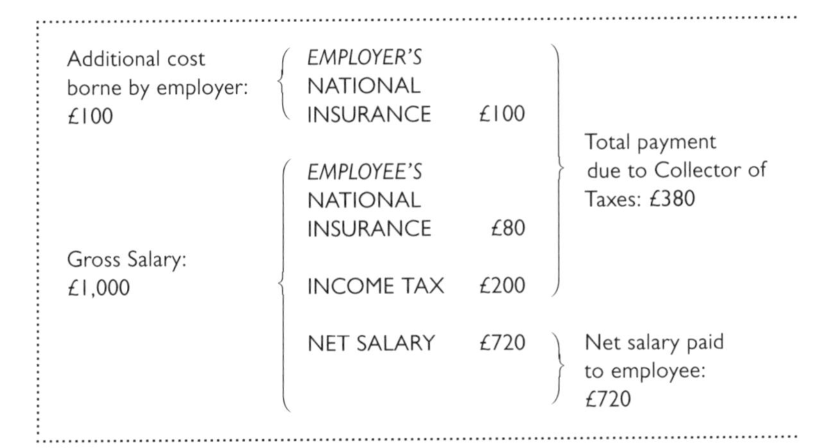

The two payments – £720 to the employee and £380 to the Collector of Taxes – add up to £1,100, which is the total cost of employing the person that month, and if both are paid immediately you will write two cheques. If you have other deductions such as pension contributions (including stakeholder pensions), or payroll giving (for donations to charity), the same general principles apply, and you may then be making three or four payments in all, for example to the:

- employee;
- HM Collector of Taxes;
- pension provider; and
- payroll giving agency.

It is generally best to post each payment as a separate entry in the books.

Some organisations like to allocate the employer's NI (and any pension contributions paid by the employer) to a different account from the gross salary in order to distinguish 'on costs' from direct salary. In order to get the correct totals, this would need the following postings (expressed in double entry format):

- £720 Net salary cheque
  - Credit: Bank £720
  - Debit: Salary expenditure £720
- £380 Collector of Taxes cheque
  - Credit: Bank £380
  - Debit: Salary expenditure £280
    Debit: Employer's NI expenditure £100

Where salary costs have to be split between two accounts – perhaps because a member of staff is splitting their time between two projects – apportion both the net salary payment and the Collector of Taxes payment on the same formula. If you want your books to be linked directly to the format of the SOFA (see chapter 7), you may also need to split salary costs between time spent on direct charitable activities as opposed to time spent on generating funds or on management and administration. But if you need to do apportionments like this, try to avoid splitting out the employer's NI as well, or the whole process could become unmanageable.

If you have several employees you can make a single payment to the Collector of Taxes, to cover the tax and NI for all staff, but if so, take care to allocate the costs for each employee to the correct expenditure accounts.

The payment to the Collector of Taxes does not have to be made until the following month, so at year end this can mean quite a large creditor is outstanding in your accounts. In fact, small organisations (in 2001/02 those whose average monthly tax and NI is less than £1500) can opt to pay the tax and NI just once a quarter, which means there will nearly always be some tax and NI waiting to be paid.

To show this properly you really need to use accruals accounting (see chapter 10) with the tax amount entered as a creditor. So in the example above, at the time of doing the payroll you would post:

- £380 Collector of Taxes amount due
  - Credit: Creditor (tax and NI): £380
  - Debit: Salary expenditure £280
  - Debit: Employer's NI expenditure £100

and then when the payment is made (possibly in the following year) the entry will be:

- £380 creditor paid by cheque to Collector of Taxes
  - Credit: Bank £380
  - Debit: Creditor (tax and NI): £380

If you don't want to get into this, the simplest way is just to pay all the tax and NI to the Collector of Taxes before the end of the month, you can then use normal payments – as in the example, on page 59) .

Posting non-bank transactions

The vast majority of transactions in your books will be receipts and payments of some kind, or possibly transfers of money between bank accounts. If you forget to enter any of these you will soon realise when you do a bank reconciliation (see chapter 7).

But some transactions arise purely from policy decisions, or from knowledge of amounts outstanding, and are thus easily overlooked. Before you close the books at the end of an accounting period, you need some means of checking with others whether any non-bank entries are needed.

A transfer between funds (see chapter 3) is, in effect, a payment from one fund and a receipt into another fund, but if the funds share the same bank account, no bank entry is involved. Or in double entry terms:

- £500 transfer from General Fund to Outreach Fund
  - Debit: General Fund expenditure 'Transfers **to** other funds' £500
  - Credit: Outreach Fund income 'Transfers ***from*** other funds' £500

It is best to post fund transfers to columns or accounts separately from other receipts and payments, so that they can be separated as inter-fund transfers on the SOFA, and are not confused with external receipts or payments.

If you are keeping accruals accounts, you will also need a wide range of other non-bank postings, in order to enter debtors, creditors, depreciation and so on (see chapter 10). With receipts and payments accounts, these do not have to be entered in the monetary books, but you still need to have some means of tracking debtors, creditors and fixed assets – a paper list may be sufficient – so you can include them on the statement of assets and liabilities (SOAL – see chapter 7).

Changing the currency of the books

One important issue to bear in mind is the possibility that at some stage the UK may join the single European currency. Whatever your personal views, if it happens the charity needs to be able to handle the changeover.

Initially you may find that coping with awkward amounts is the biggest challenge: a regular incoming donation of £20.00 per month might change to something awkward like €31.59 (the actual conversion rate will be fixed, but will involve up to six decimal places, so rounding will be needed).

Local charities will not need multi-currency accounting: you would simply change everything from pounds to euro as from a certain date (use the same date as when your bank account is converted – for countries that joined the euro at the outset, the changeover date was 1 January 2002). But bear in mind the changeover date may not coincide with your accounting year end. All reports after the changeover will need to be in euro, even though they may partly include periods when you were still working in pounds. Even after the change, you would probably still receive some cash donations in sterling.

Changing from keeping accounts in pounds to euro will obviously have a huge effect on the accounts in any kind of organisation, and there will be plenty of guidance and the experience of other countries at the time. But it may only be a few years away, and if you are setting up new books or a new computer system, it is worth building this into your plans.

6 Checks and controls

Bookkeeping procedures, as discussed in the last chapter, are only useful if people are confident about them. A key question for the trustees of any charity (and for its donors, funders, members and others) is 'do the books properly record all the income due to the charity and all expenditure as agreed by the trustees?'.

To some extent this will be answered at year end by the charity's independent examiner or auditor – see chapter 8. But examiners and auditors rely heavily on the internal controls built into your own systems: if you want your auditors to examine every single item of expenditure individually and check whether it has been approved by trustees and posted to the correct fund, you will have to pay an astronomical audit fee. Moreover, if there are problems in the books, you want to know about them before year end; for example if a fraud was going on but was not uncovered until after year end, a great deal of money could have been lost. At a lesser level, any treasurer or bookkeeper will make occasional mistakes, and the more these can be picked up through simple checks, the better the quality of the financial information obtained from the accounts.

Approval of expenditure

In a tiny charity, every payment might be discussed individually at a trustees' meeting, and the cheques written and signed at the meeting. But most organisations need to delegate decisions for approving day to day expenses and writing cheques.

However, these procedures need to be clear and robust, otherwise there is a serious risk of the charity's funds being spent on non-charitable purposes or on costs that are not intended or agreed. Moreover, with multiple funds (see chapter 3) you need to ensure that expenditure is considered separately in relation to each relevant fund, and then posted to the correct fund in the books.

A basic requirement now widely accepted in charitable organisations of all sizes is to ensure that all cheques have to be signed by two people –

normally this will be two trustees, although the trustees can nominate a senior member of staff as one signatory.

But having cheques signed by two people only offers protection if both signatories give careful thought before signing. For one person to pre-sign cheques before they are completed, or even to sign completed cheques without any real thought, offers no protection at all. Suppose you are the second trustee authorised to sign cheques and the treasurer presents you a cheque for countersignature, it is worth asking these questions before signing:

- Is the cheque to pay a definite bill or invoice? If so, be sure you see the bill and check the amount and the payee before signing.
- Does the bill relate to expenditure of a kind the trustees have approved? If not, wait until the issue can be discussed at a trustees' meeting.
- If the cheque is for a payment with no invoice, such as wages or salaries, is the amount reasonable? (You need to know salary scales of the staff concerned.) Depending on the deductions, salary payments tend to be for awkward amounts, but from time to time you should ask to check the PAYE calculations. If there are two payments, one to the employee and one to the Collector of Taxes, look at the total of the two. If a salary payment is increased because of overtime or a pay rise, make sure you see the paperwork.
- Before signing for standing orders or direct debits, be sure that the trustees have agreed the relevant payment on an ongoing basis. With direct debits, where your supplier can vary the charge, is there a proper procedure to check that the amounts actually going through the bank are correct?
- With cheques for petty cash, always insist on seeing the petty cash records explaining how the previous petty cash was spent. Be very suspicious if someone tells you that extra large amounts of petty cash are needed – what are the reasons, and how will the cash be controlled?
- Even if the expenditure looks reasonable in principle, does it fall within agreed budgets (see chapter 9)?
- Even if the expenditure is apparently reasonable, is it appropriate for the fund concerned? For example, an older people's project might have a budget for 'equipment' but if you are asked to sign cheques for children's play equipment, you might be suspicious. (Bills should always be marked to show where the cost will be allocated, before asking anyone to countersign a cheque.)

- Have you already signed a cheque for the same item? This could just be an oversight, but some frauds rely on making payments twice and then diverting the second payment. If there are several co-signatories this needs care – you may want to look back through the cheque book.

However, look at the expenditure arrangements as a whole – there is no point in having thorough checks on the payment of small bills unless your controls are just as strict for paying salaries. Where a member of staff is basically responsible for his or her own salary computations, regular checks are vital. If, as treasurer, you don't really understand PAYE and you leave it to a member of staff, the trustees are taking great risks.

Some organisations find it difficult to get two signatories that include at least one trustee, and they try to find ways round it. But provided you have three or four signatories (on an 'any two out of four' basis), you should usually be able to get cheques signed within a few days, even if they have to go by post between signatories.

All payments should be approved by two independent signatories, so for payments such as reimbursing trustees' expenses, the trustee being paid should not be one of the signatories (unless that specific payment has been discussed by the trustees as a whole).

Where small payments have to be made urgently, petty cash is one solution, but an alternative is to open a small bank account where cheques up to a small amount can be signed purely by a member of staff. This will be topped up from time to time by transfers from the main account; in such cases the main control is when making transfers from the main account, on the same lines as when drawing petty cash.

Alternatively, larger charities may be able to get their banks to agree mandates whereby cheques up to a certain level can be signed purely by two staff, with trustee signatures only required on larger amounts. But you must ensure such arrangements are permitted by your governing document; if your constitution or trust deed says 'all cheques must be signed by two trustees' you must keep to this.

Control of income

For charities whose income consists of a small number of large grants, the main issue is controlling expenditure. But in charities where much of the income comes from ad hoc donations, there is a huge risk of funds being lost because of donations not being banked into the charity's bank account in the first place.

The risk is greatest with incoming cash. If you have cash collections – for example collections at religious services or community events – try to ensure that the money is within sight of at least two people from the moment it is given, until it is counted and signed for. You need some kind of record form, signed by both people at the time the cash is counted. With other kinds of collections – in the street or with static boxes – it is best to use collecting boxes with a seal, and have a clear rule that there must be two people present when the seal is removed and the box opened.

Even incoming cheques present risks. If the charity's name is often abbreviated to initials, it is not that difficult for someone dishonest to alter the payee and pay the cheque into a personal account. This risk is much greater in charities than in commercial businesses, because a customer of a business who sends in a cheque is likely to complain if they do not get what they ordered, but people who send donations to charities rarely complain if they get no response. More serious cases of fraud have involved dishonest treasurers opening an additional bank account in the charity's name, not known to the other trustees or the auditor, and diverting substantial funds through that account.

Many charities that receive ad hoc donations thus try to arrange for all incoming post to be opened with two people present. This can be difficult in a very small organisation, but if you can only manage one person, try to vary the person, have a strict rule on recording all donations as soon as the post is opened, and make regular spot checks.

Control of income is also about making sure the charity actually receives all the income promised: if you have donors or funders making promises of future support, you need a system to check that what is received corresponds (at least) to what was promised – some organisations are very lax about sending reminders. With anyone making a regular gift, it is always worth enquiring if the gifts suddenly stop – the person may still wish to give and it could just be an error by their bank. With funding from trusts or public sector grants, where grants are paid in instalments, the charity normally has to complete a monitoring or claim form to receive the second and subsequent instalments: amazingly some charities actually fail to make these claims.

Honesty

Clearly no system of checks can be absolutely secure, particularly in a small organisation, and the first point of control is to ensure that all trustees and all staff involved with the finances of the charity are honest and dependable. With staff, taking up references is important. Similarly, if someone relatively new to an organisation volunteers to become treasurer, it is worth enquiring about the person's background, and perhaps seeking a reference from any previous charity with which he or she been involved.

In many organisations honesty is taken for granted, and sometimes treasurers feel threatened if they are asked to have a witness when counting cash or when the second signatory asks questions before signing a cheque. There is an assumption in much of the voluntary sector, and especially in religious organisations, that honesty is so fundamental to the organisation's beliefs that independent checks are unnecessary.

However, as many organisations know to their cost, even those with the most noble aims sometimes get led astray. Quite apart from the risk of fraud, a second person looking at cheques and receipts reduces the risk of error. Also, even the most honest treasurers sometimes get months behind with their books if no one asks to see them: the charity as a whole needs a means of picking up signs when a treasurer is no longer coping and needs help or needs to step down.

Verifying the books

Proper control of income and expenditure is the first step, but you then need to be sure that what is recorded in the books corresponds to what has been agreed. Even the most honest person will make occasional errors, and you need the means to identify these and correct them. There have been cases where, either through fraud or incompetence, the books completely fail to reflect the actual monies coming in and out.

Bank reconciliation

One of the most important checks is to do a bank reconciliation every time a bank statement is received. Whilst this doesn't prove everything in the books is correct, it does give a strong confirmation that what has been posted to the bank account in the books of the charity corresponds to what has physically gone through the bank. If you have several bank accounts, you need to do this for each account, and you need to ensure bank statements are received frequently enough so that if a discrepancy is found you have a reasonable chance of finding the cause (normally you will want a monthly statement on your main current account).

Of course, bank reconciliation is only possible if you are maintaining a bank balance in your books, that can be cross checked. Your own figure could be in a 'bank' column in an analysed cashbook (see chapter 5), or in a separate bank ledger (for example in a computer system) or, in a very small organisation, the running bank balance could just be maintained as a running cheque book balance (provided you have a cashbook as well, to analyse the purpose of each receipt or payment).

In general the bank balance in the books will not correspond to the balance on the bank statement because of the issue of uncleared cheques (also known as 'unpresented' cheques). For example, suppose you wrote a cheque for £50 to Jane Smith on 15 January. If she had not paid it into her own account by about 28 January, it will not appear on your bank statement dated 31 January. In your books, you would have deducted the payment on 15 January, when you wrote the cheque, but at 31 January the money is still in the charity's bank account. If this was the only case, the balance on the bank statement would thus be £50 higher than the balance in your books.

The same problem can also apply with receipts if they were paid in just before the statement date.

In order to allow for uncleared items, you need a means of marking in your books when each cheque, receipt, or any other bank transaction has actually cleared – many people put a tick against the cheque in their books and on the statement (and computer-based accounting systems often have a means to do this automatically).

You then need to go through the books, noting all uncleared items (which could be in any fund which uses the bank account concerned). Add up the uncleared cheques, and the uncleared receipts if you have any. Remember to include items still uncleared from previous months – in some cases this may mean going back to last year's accounts. You can then set down a bank reconciliation calculation (see figure 6.1).

Figure 6.1 Bank reconciliation

Bank reconciliation – Current account as at 31 January

BALANCE OF ACCOUNT AS ON BANK STATEMENT:			£2,236.75
Less uncleared cheques:			
	000274	15.00	
	000276	678.00	
		693.00	–693.00
Plus uncleared receipts:	None		+0.00
Expected balance in books:			£1,543.75
ACTUAL BALANCE OF BANK ACCOUNT IN BOOKS:			£1,543.75

If the expected balance from the calculation ties up with the actual balance recorded in your books, this is a good confirmation of your bookkeeping. If there is a discrepancy, work out the difference between the two figures, and look for an error of that amount. The possible causes of bank reconciliation errors must always come down to one or more of the following:

- a payment or receipt entered in the books is marked as cleared, but in fact it has not yet gone through the bank;
- a payment or receipt is not marked in the books as cleared when in fact it has appeared on the statement;
- an item on the bank statement that has not been entered in the books (look especially at interest payments, direct debits, bank charges, transfers between accounts, incoming standing orders);
- an item that has been entered in the books twice;
- an item that was entered in the books as a payment but it was actually a receipt (or vice versa) – if so, the discrepancy on reconciliation will be twice the amount of the item;
- an item that appears in the books and on the bank statement, but the amounts are different, usually due to a clerical error (this takes a lot of time to spot – get someone to call out the statement while you check the books, or vice versa);
- if you have several bank accounts, an item that has been posted in the books to the wrong account;
- a calculation error in the running balance in the books.

If the reconciliation was correct the previous month, the problem must be something in the books that has changed since then. But remember that when you mark the books for items that are now cleared, you will often be marking prior months' entries as well as those for the current month. So in considering what has changed since the previous month, you may be looking at several months' entries.

Other checks on the books

With petty cash, the main check is simply to count the actual amount of petty cash regularly, to be sure it corresponds with the expected value in the books. If not, is it a clerical error, or has someone been taking petty cash without authority? If the balance in the cash tin is higher than expected – not unknown in charities – it could be because of people putting donations in the tin. It is best to make some other arrangement for cash donations.

With the accounts for the different categories of income and expenditure, physical checks are rarely possible: the main test is one of reasonableness. This is where budgets help enormously: if a given account is heavily over or under budget, is there a good reason, or is it because receipts or payments have been posted correctly as far as the bank account is concerned, but allocated to the wrong income or expenditure category?

With multiple funds, it is particularly important to be certain that all income and expenses are allocated to the correct fund, otherwise restricted funds (see chapter 3) may be used for the wrong purposes. Some regular sample checks of this kind by someone other than the treasurer or bookkeeper can help to pick up problems at an early stage.

Subsidiary groups

Many charities have subsidiary groups that handle their own money on a day to day basis, but which are legally part of the main charity.

It is important to remember that money under the control of such groups is part of the funds for which the charity trustees are responsible, and at year end these figures must be included with the 'main' accounts, in order to produce proper year end accounts for the whole charity.

Make sure that such groups have reasonable controls to prevent money belonging to the charity from going astray, and ensure that charity money is not being held in personal accounts. If such groups have their own bank account, check that proper procedures are followed for cheque signatories and bank reconciliation. To prevent groups harbouring funds that no one knows about, it is worth having a rule that no bank account can be opened by any group without approval by the trustees.

7 Final accounts

For many treasurers and finance officers, producing the year end accounts is the most demanding task of the year. But although you will probably be quite busy in the weeks immediately after year end, if you have been keeping good books and maintaining adequate controls, the year end process can actually be quite rewarding, as you see your work come to fruition, and put into a form for digestion by the outside world.

Obviously the work will be considerably less if your books are structured in a way that links closely to the year end accounts. If you are using computer software designed to generate reports in line with the Regulations and SORP, the task is simpler still.

Who are the accounts for?

Although several chapters of this book are concerned with the legal requirements for the accounts, it is important to remember that your final accounts are much more than a document to meet charity law.

Companies in business sometimes produce the briefest possible accounts that comply with the law, in order to avoid disclosing too much to their competitors. But for a charity, the opposite usually applies: your annual accounts are a key means of communication with members, funders and supporters (present and future), and you will often want to include more than the legal minimum. Your accounts may also go to umbrella bodies to which you are affiliated, to the Inland Revenue, to Companies House (if your organisation is a charitable company), and elsewhere. If you are applying for grants, your prospective funders may read your accounts much more closely than the Charity Commission. However, you also want to avoid giving so much detail that readers cannot see the overall picture. To a large extent the legal requirements help in this, by requiring a certain degree of standardisation in the accounts of all charities.

Before preparing a set of accounts for the first time, or before making a major change to the current format, it is worth thinking about all the audiences you are aiming at. An annual competition called the *Charities' Annual Report and Accounts Annual Awards* run by the Charities Aid Foundation (see *Useful addresses*) highlights some of the best examples.

It is also worth noting that in principle you could produce different sorts of accounts for different audiences: for example, some larger charities produce full accounts for the Charity Commission and for those supporters who want the full detail, and summarised accounts for others. However, for a smaller charity, this is a lot of extra work, the summarised accounts must make clear that they are only a summary, and must include a statement by your auditor or independent examiner that they are not inconsistent with the full accounts. Most local charities find that those supporters who want accounts really want the full detail, and others are not really interested in accounts at all!

Similarly, a charitable company could in theory produce one set of accounts complying with the SORP to send to the Charity Commission, and another set complying with the Companies Acts to send to Companies House. But in practice, it is much less work to produce one set of accounts that meet the requirements of both charity law and company law.

What about the annual report?

In law, a charity must produce two public documents at year end – the *annual report* and the *annual accounts*. Each must be approved and signed by the trustees before they can be circulated, and in most cases the accounts must have an auditor's or independent examiner's report (see chapter 8). They can be printed or copied separately, but anyone requesting the accounts must also be given the annual report and vice versa, so it is usually best to combine them into one document called the 'annual report and accounts'.

The treasurer is usually responsible for arranging the preparation of the annual accounts, but it may be that someone else in the charity – perhaps the secretary or chief officer – will draft the annual report. However, in such cases, there needs to be a good deal of liaison, particularly on aspects of the annual report dealing with financial issues, such as comments on the financial performance for the year, and a statement of the reserves policy (see chapter 4).

Table 7.1 Charity annual reports – summary of requirements

Factual section

(a) Official name of the charity (and any working names)
(b) Registered charity number (if registered)
(c) Official address of the charity
(d) Particulars of governing document
(e) Description of the (objects) of the charity. Usually this is easily obtained from the constitution or other governing document
(f) Any external persons* or bodies entitled to appoint trustees to the charity
(g) List of the names* of all trustees at the date of approving the report
(h) Names* of all other trustees who served for any part of the financial year
(i) Names* of custodian trustees at date of approval
(j) Any other custodian trustees* during year

*If disclosing trustees' names would put anyone in personal danger, the charity can apply to Charity Commission for permission to omit them.

Narrative section

- If the total income was £250,000 or under: a brief review of the main activities and achievements of the charity in relation to its objects.
- If the total income was over £250,000: describe all activities in relation to the objects including any material transactions and significant developments and changes in the year; important events since year end; and the organisational structure.

Policies section

Description of any policies adopted by trustees for:

- Level of reserves
- Investment policy
- Grant-making policy

Extras needed for charities over £250,000 income

- Risk assessment
- Action being taken on funds in deficit
- Investment performance

This is a summary – for full details see regulation 7 of Charities (Accounts and Reports Regulations) 2000.

It is not possible in this book to cover the full requirements for annual reports, but table 7.1 gives a summary. It may fall to you as treasurer to ensure the other trustees are aware of these requirements.

In the case of a charitable company, it is usual to provide one report that is both the directors' annual report required under company law, and the trustees' annual report required under charity law. This dual requirement is sometimes overlooked: a report that only covers the requirements of the Companies Acts is not sufficient. Furthermore, a report that fails to give a proper review of the charity's activities can be disastrous when applying for funding.

The annual report must be a report by the trustees as a whole. Some charities like to produce an attractive document with reports by key individuals, comments by participants or users, photographs and much more. With care on the wording, this can be incorporated into the legal annual report, but often it is easier to issue this kind of material as a separate document called an *annual review*.

Who prepares the accounts?

The term 'preparing the accounts' means taking the information from the books, and turning them into a final document which, once approved and signed by the trustees, can be copied and circulated. Nowadays the document is usually created by word processing, so a draft can easily be amended (but in principle, for a very small charity, the document could still be hand-written or typewritten).

Except in the very smallest organisations, your accounts will then be subject to audit or independent examination (see chapter 8). So it is usual to involve your auditor or examiner while the accounts are still in draft. Depending on the complexity of the accounts and the relative experience in preparing accounts, there are four main ways of sharing the work.

(a) Auditor/examiner appointed only to report
In this 'pure audit' model, the charity produces final accounts complying with the regulations etc.; these accounts are approved and signed by trustees. They are then submitted to the auditor/examiner for scrutiny and report.

(b) Auditor/examiner may request amendments and then reports
In this approach, the charity produces draft final accounts including the full notes. These are submitted to the auditor/examiner for provisional approval or to request amendment. The amendments are then

incorporated and the accounts signed by trustees. The auditor/examiner then attaches and signs his or her report.

(c) Auditor/examiner completes accounts and then reports
The charity produces the basis of the accounts – perhaps the main financial reports from an accounting system and a summary of items for the notes. The auditor/examiner then turns these into a full set of accounts. These (externally finalised) accounts are presented to the charity and signed by the trustees, and the auditor/examiner then signs his or her report.

(d) Auditor/examiner produces accounts from scratch and reports on them
In charities with very limited financial experience, it often happens that the charity provides the auditor/examiner purely with the books. From these, the examiner/auditor prepares a full set of accounts from scratch. These (externally prepared) accounts are signed by the trustees and the auditor/examiner then signs his or her report.

Which approach to use?

If possible, approach (b) or (c) is best. These allow a proper dialogue between the charity and the auditor or examiner. The main difference between them is that in (b) the charity does the word processing of the final document and the auditor/examiner requests changes; in (c) it is the other way round.

Although approach (a) can work with very small organisations, the problem is that if the auditor/examiner is unhappy with anything in the accounts, there is no alternative but to issue a qualified report (an audit or examination report that contains qualifications or reservations). It can be quite damaging to the charity to have to circulate accounts with a qualified auditor's/examiner's report. If a small amendment to the accounts – perhaps adding an extra note – would have solved the problem, it is much better to be able to incorporate this before final approval by the trustees.

The main problem with approach (d) is that if someone outside the charity does almost everything, will your trustees be able to make a sensible decision about approving the accounts? Remember that in law, producing the accounts is the responsibility of the charity trustees. It is fine for the trustees to use an accountant to help prepare the accounts, but the trustees are responsible for the content.

For example, if the books didn't properly distinguish a restricted fund (because the bookkeeper included a special grant with general donations) there is no way an accountant could know this unless told. If accounts are prepared showing money in the general fund that should be restricted, it is up to the trustees to spot this when considering the approval of the accounts, and ask for the draft to be changed before they sign.

Many charities get into the circular argument of saying 'these accounts have been prepared by our accountants so they must be correct' and then the accountant (now acting as auditor/examiner) says 'since the accounts have been approved by the trustees, the content must be OK' and each is signing on the basis of an assumption of what the other has done.

The content of the final accounts

As explained in chapter 2, there are two possible formats for the final accounts: receipts and payments and accruals – which has to comply with the SORP.

Note that these are the only formats permitted by law in England, Wales and Scotland (the law is less precise in Northern Ireland). Mixtures of receipts and payments and accruals, and other formats from the past will not generally meet the needs of charity law.

The rest of this chapter explains the general framework. But preparing final accounts, particularly accruals accounts in SORP format, involves much more than can be covered in a book of this length. There are plenty of books giving more detailed advice – see *Further reading*. Figures 7.1 and 7.2 illustrate the formats you will commonly see (but beware of using these examples as models for one simple charity, because different information may be needed in different charities).

Final receipts and payments accounts

The Charities Act 1993 says that when a charity opts to produce receipts and payments accounts, the trustees must provide:

- a receipts and payments account (which must distinguish the different funds of the charity); and
- a statement of assets and liabilities (SOAL).

In Scotland, the SOAL is replaced by a 'statement of balances' but the idea is very similar.

Figure 7.1 Example Receipts and Payments Accounts

MIDSHAM COMMUNITY ASSOCIATION – ACCOUNTS FO

RECEIPTS AND PAYMENTS ACCOUNT AND FUND MOVEMENTS 01 APR 01 TO 31 MAR 02

General Fund (Unrestricted Fund)

01 Apr 00 – 31 Mar 01 £			01 Apr 01 – 31 Mar 02 £
	Receipts		
467		Members' Subscriptions	534
10,000		Council Grant	25,000
500		Miscellaneous Donations	429
0		Tax Reclaimed on Gift Aid	140
1,103		Christmas Bazaar	1,732
71		Bank Interest	53
12,141	TOTAL RECEIPTS		27,888
	Payments		
980		Administrator Salary	1,079
934		Heat & Light	869
389		Rates, Water Rates, Cleaning	403
6,981		Repairs & Maintenance	3,708
321		Stationery	291
783		Publicity Literature	1,781
1,089		Postage & Telephone	1,237
0		Purchase of Minibus	18,000
200		Independent Examiner's Fee	200
171		Committee Travel Expenses	126
0		Contribution to Outreach Project	100
11,848	TOTAL PAYMENTS		27,794
293	SURPLUS		94
80	Balance brought forward 01 Apr 01		373
373	Balance carried forward 31 Mar 02		467

RECEIPTS AND PAYMENTS ACCOUNT AND FUND MOVEMENTS 01 APR 01 TO 31 MAR 02

Outreach Project (Restricted Fund)

01 Apr 00– 31 Mar 01 £			01 Apr 01 – 31 Mar 02 £
	Receipts		
0		Grant from Midsham Trust	4,000
0		Participants Activity Fees	713
0		Contribution from General Fund	100
0	TOTAL RECEIPTS		4,813
	Payments		
0		Outreach Worker Wages	2,760
0		Outreach Travel Costs	452
0		Outreach Activities	1,342
0	TOTAL PAYMENTS		4,554
0	SURPLUS		259
0	Balance brought forward 01 Apr 01		0
0	Balance carried forward 31 Mar 02		259

THE YEAR ENDING 31 MARCH 2002 (Receipts and Payments Format)

STATEMENT OF ASSETS AND LIABILITIES AT 31 MAR 02

31 Mar 01 *£*		31 Mar 02 £
	Monetary Assets	
	Current Asset Investments	
250	Investment Acct – Midwest Bank	690
	Cash At Bank and In Hand	
114	Current Account – Midwest Bank	20
9	Petty Cash	16
123	Total Cash At Bank and In Hand	36
373	TOTAL MONETARY ASSETS	726
	Represented by Funds	
	Unrestricted Funds	
373	General Fund	467
	Restricted Funds	
0	Outreach Project	259
373	TOTAL FUNDS	726
	Non-Monetary Assets & Liabilities	
	Fixed Assets for Charity Use	
120,000	Community Centre	120,000
0	Minibus	18,000
2,000	Furniture & Equipment	1,800
122,000	Total Fixed Assets for Charity Use	139,800
	Debtors	
140	Tax due from Inland Revenue	170
	Creditors Due Within One Year	
–200	Independent Examination Fee Due	–250
121,940	TOTAL NON-MONETARY ASSETS	139,720

These accounts were approved by the Trustees on 23 May 2002 and signed on their behalf by:
K PATEL – Chairperson
J CORRIGAN – Treasurer

NOTES TO THE ACCOUNTS

1. These accounts are prepared on a receipts and payments basis, with all revenue and expenses shown on a cash basis. Non-monetary assets and liabilities are shown at estimates of the value at the end of the year.
2. The charity has two funds: an unrestricted General Fund and an Outreach Project. The latter is a restricted fund supported mainly by a grant from the Midsham Trust, enabling the charity to employ a P/T outreach worker to visit families in two particular wards with high levels of disadvantage. As a condition of the funding application, the charity itself provided £100 towards this project: this is shown as a transfer from General Fund to the Outreach Fund.
3. All bank interest is allocated to the General Fund.
4. No remuneration was paid to any trustee. Travel expenses totalling £176 were paid to four trustees: £126 of this was from the General Fund, and £50 from the Outreach Project Fund.

Receipts and payments accounts

In England and Wales, there are no rules in law about how the receipts and payments account is to be laid out, so you are free to break down the receipts and payments into whatever categories you feel would be helpful to your readers. However, the Charity Commission publishes some very useful guidance, and there are also a few pages in the 2000 SORP regarding receipts and payments accounts. It is normal to include a comparative column for the previous year, which means trying to keep the same categories from year to year.

Where there are several funds, you can show a completely separate receipts and payments account for each fund, as in figure 7.1 (if so, it is more readable if you use a separate page for each fund). But if there are more than about three funds, and particularly if there have been transfers between funds, it may be clearer to show all funds together in a SOFA-type layout (see figure 7.2), so long as it is clearly labelled as being on a 'receipts and payments basis'. However, if several funds are added together into one column, a note explaining the different funds is clearly needed.

The statement of assets and liabilities (SOAL)

The SOAL must list all the assets and liabilities of the charity: it is easiest to divide this into the monetary assets (which will correspond to the balances of funds) and other, non-monetary, assets and liabilities such as fixed assets, debtors and creditors. In principle the non-monetary assets could just be presented as a list of items, but if you have estimates of values it is sensible to show them.

Hopefully, as treasurer you will know about any unpaid bills and amounts due to the charity and will thus be able to work out the debtors and creditors, and you will know about new capital items bought during the year. But the fixed assets must include all long term items owned by the charity (including items acquired or given many years previously), and if no one has produced one before, you may have to compile a fixed asset list from scratch. Don't forget to include buildings and investments, as well as obvious items of furniture, equipment and vehicles. Also, ask if there are any long-standing loans or other commitments: these will need to appear as liabilities on the SOAL.

From this it is clear that even with receipts and payments accounting, the task of the treasurer is more than just keeping track of the money: you must know about fixed assets, debtors and creditors even if these do not actually appear in the day to day books. But once you have produced the SOAL for one year, you can produce it quite easily in future years by altering each value for the net movement in the relevant non-monetary items.

Notes to the accounts

With receipts and payments accounts, there are no legal requirements to show notes to the accounts, but in practice your accounts will be much more meaningful to readers if you include relevant information by way of notes. The list of notes needed for accruals accounts (see table 7.2) is a good starting point. You won't need all of these, but notes explaining the purpose of each fund and any payments to trustees are good practice whatever the size of the charity.

Final accruals accounts

Once you move on to accruals accounts, the figures will be slightly different because debtors, creditors and fixed assets are included in the fund balances. (Generally this is compulsory for charities over £100,000 income, but see chapter 2 for details.) Furthermore, accruals accounts must be presented in accordance with the Regulations, which means using 'SORP format'. So the accounts will consist of:

- a statement of financial activities (SOFA);
- a balance sheet;
- notes to the accounts.

The rules are quite specific about the principles and layout of the SOFA and balance sheet, and on information that must be given in the notes to the accounts. There are some minor concessions for charities with income £250,000 or below, but in general once a charity issues accruals accounts, the full SORP presentation must be used.

Figure 7.2 Example Accruals Accounts

MIDSHAM COMMUNITY ASSOCIATION – ACCOUNTS FO

STATEMENT OF FINANCIAL ACTIVITIES 01 APR 01 TO 31 MAR 02

	01 Apr 01 – 31 Mar 02				*01 Apr 00 – 31 Mar 01*
	Unrestricted Funds £	Restricted Funds £	Capital Funds £	Total Funds £	*All Funds £*
Incoming Resources					
Donations, Gifts, Grants	25,599	4,000		29,599	*10,500*
Services Provided for Char Obj	534	713		1,247	*467*
Sales from Fundraising Activs	1,732			1,732	*1,103*
Investment Income	53			53	*71*
Total Incoming Resources	27,918	4,713	0	32,631	*12,141*
Resources Expended					
Cost of Generating Funds	1,781			1,781	*783*
Grants Payable Under Char Objs				0	*0*
Activities Furthering Char Obj	9,680	4,554		14,234	*8,304*
Support Costs	291			291	*321*
Management & Admin of Charity	2,692			2,692	*2,440*
Total Resources Used	14,444	4,554	0	18,998	*11,848*
NET RESOURCES BEFORE TRANSFERS	13,474	159	0	13,633	*293*
Transfers Between Funds					
Miscellaneous Transfers	–100	100		0	*0*
NET MOVEMENT IN FUNDS	13,374	259	0	13,633	*293*
Fund Balances Brought Forward 01 Apr 01	2,313	0	120,000	122,313	*122,020*
Fund Balances Carried Forward 31 Mar 02	15,687	259	120,000	135,946	*122,313*

The notes on page 3 to 6 form part of these accounts.

NOTES TO THE ACCOUNTS

This example does not show the notes – however, as these are accruals accounts, full notes covering all the issues required by the regulations and SORP will be needed on the pages after the Balance Sheet. In a simple charity such as this, the notes might include:

1. Accounting policies.
2. Description of each fund and explanation of inter-fund transfers.
3. Summary of movements on each fund (this would be needed if more than one fund included in any column of the SOFA).
4. Table of fixed asset movements showing additions, depreciation etc, for each type of assets.
5. Explanation of debtors (unless fully shown on Balance Sheet).
6. Explanation of creditors (unless fully shown on Balance Sheet).
7. Details of staff numbers and salary costs.
8. Explanation of trustees expenses, and a statement that there were no other transactions with trustees.
9. Note of independent examiner's fee.
10. Estimate of market value of the land occupied by the Community Centre.
11. Details of any long-term commitments made.

The notes also need to include last year's comparisons where applicable.

'HE YEAR ENDING 31 MARCH 2002 (Accruals Basis – SORP Format)

BALANCE SHEET AT 31 MAR 02

	31 Mar 02 £	*31 Mar 01 £*
Assets and Liabilities		
FIXED ASSETS		
Fixed Assets for Charity Use		
Community Centre	120,000	*120,000*
Minibus	13,500	*0*
Furniture & Equipment	1,800	*2,000*
Total Fixed Assets for Charity Use	135,300	*122,000*
CURRENT ASSETS		
Debtors		
Tax due from Inland Revenue	170	*140*
Current Asset Investments		
Investment Acct – Midwest Bank	690	*250*
Cash At Bank and In Hand		
Current Account – Midwest Bank	20	*114*
Petty Cash	16	*9*
Total Cash At Bank and In Hand	36	*123*
	896	*513*
CURRENT LIABILITIES		
Creditors Due Within One Year		
Independent Examination Fee Due	250	*200*
NET CURRENT ASSETS	646	*313*
TOTAL ASSETS LESS CURRENT LIABILITIES	135,946	*122,313*
NET ASSETS	135,946	*122,313*
Represented by Funds		
Unrestricted Funds		
General Fund	15,687	*2,313*
Restricted Funds		
Outreach Project	259	*0*
Capital Funds		
Buildings Reserve	120,000	*120,000*
TOTAL FUNDS	135,946	*122,313*

Approved by the Trustees on 23 May 2002 and signed on their behalf by:
K PATEL – Chairperson
J CORRIGAN – Treasurer

NOTES TO THE ACCOUNTS
(These will follow on subsequent pages – see box opposite.)

The statement of financial activities

The SOFA is essentially an income and expenditure account divided into columns for the three types of funds: unrestricted funds (this includes designated funds); restricted income funds; and capital or endowment funds (see chapter 3 for definitions). There is a column showing the total income and expenditure of all funds, and a comparison column with the overall totals for the last year.

The SOFA can seem complex at first, but once people get used to it, it is actually a very helpful way of understanding the income and expenditure of an organisation, without confusing restricted and unrestricted funds, but showing the whole charity on one page. There is a separate line for any transfers between funds, so support from one fund to another is not confused with external income or expenditure – see chapters 3 and 4 for more on this. This line must, of course, total to zero in the 'All funds' column, because the transfers out of one fund must be balanced by transfers into other funds. Sometimes the SOFA will include a further section for gains and losses where assets are revalued, but this is not shown in figure 7.2.

Within each column there may be several funds added together – for example the second column could have the totals for ten or more projects supported by restricted funds – but notes to the accounts must give individual balances for each fund.

As well as specifying the columns, the SORP rules specify the general headings to be used for income and expenditure, in order to ensure comparability between different charities.

For full SORP format, the expenditure must be broken down on a functional basis, showing how much was spent on particular purposes. So, rather than having a single line for 'salaries', salary costs for fundraising come under 'Cost of generating funds', time spent on the main work of the charity appears under 'Activities furthering the charitable objects' and staff time used in, for example, supporting the trustees, internal accounting, organising AGMs, is included in 'Management and administration of the charity'. In a medium charity, this may mean splitting the salaries of individual staff.

If this seems too hard, charities with income £250,000 or below are allowed to use natural classifications of expenditure on the SOFA (for example 'Salaries', 'Premises', 'Running costs', 'Depreciation') to simplify things. But you must still break down the income side according to the prescribed categories in the SORP (figure 7.2 abbreviates these).

The balance sheet

The balance sheet shows all the charity's assets and liabilities, balanced against the relevant funds. The key thing to appreciate with accruals accounts is that the value of every fixed asset, debtor or creditor is included in the relevant fund (unlike receipts and payments accounts, where the fund balances comprise only of money). See chapter 10 for more on this.

The top half of the balance sheet is similar to the format used for business accounts, but the bottom half is quite different because all the assets and liabilities belong to the charity. All assets are either held for the general objects of the charity (unrestricted funds), or they are held for certain restricted or capital purposes.

Like the SOFA, the content and layout of the balance sheet is laid down by the Regulations and SORP. One key requirement is that any investments and property must be shown at market value (rather than at their original cost).

The balance sheet must be signed by the trustees to show that they have approved the accounts.

Notes to the accounts

Unlike receipts and payments accounts, where notes are at the discretion of the charity concerned, with accruals accounts it is a legal requirement to provide a great deal of additional information in notes to the accounts. All the points shown in table 7.2 must be covered by notes, if there is anything applicable.

Whilst an appropriate accounting system can help to produce the SOFA, balance sheet and one or two key notes, most of the task of preparing the notes is best done by word processing. Although the rules state what is required in the notes, the charity is free to choose the wording: if you are using a professional accountant to help prepare the accounts, try to ensure that the notes are worded in a language that will make sense to other readers. You can always give more information than the legal minimum if it will help readers understand what the charity is doing.

It usually takes several pages to cover all these issues, so the shortest SORP-compliant accounts tend to be around five pages: the SOFA, balance sheet and three or more pages of notes.

Table 7.2 Accruals accounts – summary of requirements for notes to the accounts

(a) Adjustments to last year's figures
(b) Accounting policies and assumptions
(c) Nature and purpose of each fund following SORP principles (normally provide a table with a line for each fund showing opening balance, income, expenditure, transfers, closing balance)
(d) Transactions with related parties (i.e. with trustees and their relatives/business partners) including trustees' expenses paid.
(e) Total staff costs
(f) Details of individual staff salaries over £50,000 (in £10k bands)
(g)* Trustees' indemnity insurance
(h) Details of capital receipts
(i) Details of transfers between funds [may be included with (c), but must *explain* transfers affecting restricted funds]
(j) Connected institutions (for example parent charities or trading subsidiaries)
(k) Details of any guarantees given to third parties
(l) Loans – to the charity (if secured on the charity's property) or loans made by the charity to others
(m) Explanation of any funds in deficit
(n) Auditor's/independent examiner's remuneration (and fees for other services provided to the charity by the auditor/examiner)
(o) Grants made – details as defined in SORP (if grants are more than 5% of charity's expenditure must give details of all grants over £1,000)
(p) Details of any ex gratia payments made
(q) Analysis of fixed assets, debtors, creditors (details as in SORP)
(r) Analysis of all material movements in fixed asset values
(may be combined with (q) – it is usual to give three separate notes:
- debtors
- creditors
- fixed assets – in categories showing additions, disposals, depreciation, revaluations)

(s) Contingent liabilities
(t) Financial commitments not shown in accounts
(u) Market value of land held by charity
(v) Previous year's figures for all the above except (i), (o) and (r)
(w)* Accounting standards used and details of any major departures
(x) Reasons for any change of accounting date
(y) Reasons if any departure from the Regulations had to be made in order for the accounts to give a true and fair view
(z) Any other information needed to give a true and fair view or to assist the user to understand the accounts.

* Not required for charities with income £250,000 or under.

Apart from (b), (c) and (d), which are compulsory in all cases, most notes can be omitted if there is genuinely nothing applicable.

This is a summary – for full details see the Schedule to the Charities (Accounts and Reports Regulations) 2000. See also the SORP 2000 for further detail on notes required.

Additional reports

In Scotland, charities doing accruals accounts must currently produce an income and expenditure account with certain classifications. Sometimes this is provided in addition to the SOFA, but in many cases careful use of appropriate SOFA headings can serve both the Scottish rules and the SORP requirements.

Likewise, a charitable company will sometimes need a separate income and expenditure account for the purposes of the Companies Acts, but except in special cases, the 'All funds' column on the SOFA will usually meet the Act's requirements.

Very large charities (those with any two of: more than £2.8 million income, more than £1.4 million assets or more than 50 employees) must also include a cashflow statement.

8 Audit and independent examination

As explained in the last chapter, your trustees are responsible for producing the annual accounts. They may seek help from an accountant or independent examiner to get them in the correct presentation but that is simply helping the trustees, it is quite different from the task of scrutinising the accounts from an independent perspective.

Except in the very smallest charities, once the accounts are complete there is a further legal requirement before they can be circulated – they must be subjected to an independent scrutiny by someone unconnected with the trustees. This person will then provide a report, which must be attached to the accounts. Many people use the term 'audit' to describe this process, but this is slightly misleading because, as we will see, there are several alternatives to a full audit.

The independent report is a vital protection for all concerned. Most funders and donors expect any organisations they support to produce independently scrutinised accounts. It is also a vital issue for the trustees themselves, because inevitably the day to day finances have to be delegated. So an independent report on the final accounts enables the trustees to have confidence in the overall position of the charity.

Forms of scrutiny

In the UK there are three possible forms of independent scrutiny for the accounts of a charity:

- independent examination;
- reporting accountant (also known as an 'audit exception report');
- full audit.

It is vital to know which of these is required, and what sort of person you can approach. Many people talk loosely about 'audited accounts' in all three cases, but now that the Charities Act draws a clear distinction between audit and independent examination, it is worth using the terms correctly.

The rules are largely based on the organisation's total income, but this is an area where the rules are different for charitable companies, and they also differ between England and Wales, and Scotland. Also, you must actually consider the largest income or expenditure of the charity for any of the last three years.

Table 8.1 sets out the current minimum requirement in law; some charities will need more. For example, although charities in England and Wales are not required under the Charities Act to have an independent examination if their income is £10,000 or below, an independent examination might still be required by their constitution, by a funder, or by the rules of any umbrella body to which they belong. Similarly, some charities whose income would normally put them clearly in the independent examination band may have a trust deed that requires a full audit. In Scotland the thresholds may well change once the CharityScotland proposals are implemented (see chapter 1).

Table 8.1 Minimum requirements for accounts scrutiny

MINIMUM PERMITTED SCRUTINY OF ACCOUNTS	Unincorporated charities: England and Wales Income/ expenditure level	Unincorporated charities: Scotland Income/ expenditure level	Charitable companies: Whole of UK Income/ expenditure level
Approval of accounts by trustees only	£0 to £10,000	Not applicable	£0 to £90,000
Independent examination	£10,000 to £250,000	£0 to £100,000	Not applicable
Reporting accountant	Not permitted	Not permitted	£90,000 to £250,000
Full audit	Over £250,000	Over £100,000	Over £250,000

There is currently no general law on the scrutiny of accounts for unincorporated charities in Northern Ireland, so trustees of Northern Irish charities are free to opt for whatever level of scrutiny they feel is appropriate (subject to requirements of funders and their own constitutions).

Approval of accounts by trustees only

In England and Wales, for unincorporated charities with income £10,000 or below, generally no independent scrutiny is required, and your trustees can simply approve the accounts themselves. This is intended to keep things simple for many small trusts and local voluntary groups with modest income.

But it is important to appreciate that there must still be a formal trustees' meeting at which the accounts are approved, and the trustees need to consider what this involves. As treasurer, you will probably have prepared the accounts and presented them to the trustees, but should they just approve them on your say? This is unwise, because no matter how much they trust you, something could have gone wrong – what if you have simply mistyped a crucial figure? There should still be at least one other trustee, not involved in the day to day bookkeeping, who goes back to the original records and considers whether the accounts are correct, before recommending their approval to the rest of the trustees.

With charitable companies this approach can, in principle, apply up to £90,000 income, provided you are able to put together proper accounts complying with the Companies Act and the Charities SORP. But your funders may not be happy with this and, in most cases, the trustees/directors will want some kind of professional help. If you are using professional accountants, you could ask them to issue a reporting accountant's report (see *Reporting accountant,* page 93).

Independent examination

Until the Charities Acts 1992 and 1993, many smaller charities had an 'informal audit' whereby someone with modest accounting knowledge was asked to look over the books and sign his or her name at the end of the accounts. But these kind of informal audits were often haphazard, with no indication of what the 'honorary auditor' had actually done. Even with accounts prepared by professional accountants, the accountants' report often said only 'These accounts have been prepared from the books and vouchers presented to us' with no opinion as to their completeness or accuracy.

Independent examination was brought in to replace the 'informal audits' of the past, by providing a scrutiny regime which would give some real certainty without requiring smaller charities to bear the cost of a full audit. In England and Wales, independent examination is usually appropriate for unincorporated charities with income in the range £10,000 to £250,000. The two main differences between independent examination and audit relate to who can act and the nature of the report attached to the accounts.

A wide range of people can potentially be independent examiners, though there are important criteria to consider, as explained below. But the task of an independent examiner is much more than just looking at the accounts to check the figures. In England and Wales the duties are laid down by s43 of the Charities Act 1993, Reg 7 of the Charities (Accounts and Reports) Regulations 1995, and by the Directions of the Charity Commissioners on the Carrying Out of an Independent Examination. (Slightly different rules apply in Scotland, currently determined by the Charities Accounts (Scotland) Regulations 1992.) No one can validly claim to have carried out an independent examination of a set of charity accounts unless they have followed all these requirements.

In England and Wales an independent examiner's report provides a 'negative assurance'. If the examination is satisfactory, the independent examiner's report declares that:

- no evidence was found of lack of accounting records;
- nor of the accounts failing to comply with the records;
- nor of accounts failing to comply with the Act;
- nor are there other matters that need to be disclosed.

However, such a declaration can only be made after following 12 stages of Charity Commission Directions, so it is not just a case of the examiner saying casually that no problems were spotted. The examiner's report has to cover a number of issues prescribed by the Regulations, so it will usually need a whole page. For most smaller charities an independent examination provides a very effective scrutiny, which goes much further than the 'informal audits' of the past, but which can be carried out without needing a registered auditor.

Selecting an independent examiner

An independent examiner is defined in law as 'an independent person who is reasonably believed by the charity trustees to have the requisite ability and practical experience to carry out a competent examination of the accounts' (this definition applies in Scotland as well as England and Wales).

No specific qualification is required, but clearly the person must have a good understanding of accounts, and charity accounts in particular. Independent examiners come from a wide range of backgrounds including accountants, bankers, engineers, staff of community accountancy projects and experienced charity treasurers acting as independent examiners to other charities. Some work professionally and thus charge a fee, but this is usually a good deal less than the cost of a full audit; however, many independent examiners, especially those acting for the smallest charities, work on a voluntary basis or charge only a nominal fee.

However, there can be certain concerns about the issues of 'requisite ability' and 'practical experience'. Even amongst accountants only a few firms specialise in charities, and others can easily be caught out by all the requirements. Where people are acting informally as independent examiners there is wide ignorance of the new regime, for example some 'informal auditors' are doing just as they did in the past but simply putting 'independent examiner' after their name – this is illegal.

The issue of independence is also very important: some 'informal audits' in the past have been carried out by funders, landlords or close relatives of trustees, where there is clearly insufficient independence. It should be noted that an independent examiner must always be an individual, there is no provision for independent examination reports to be signed by a firm.

Whilst there is no legal requirement to have any specific qualification in order to be an independent examiner, Charity Commission guidance stresses the need for trustees to check that a prospective independent examiner really does have the appropriate competence. One factor that is becoming a strong indicator in this respect is the MACIE qualification, denoting Full Membership of the Association of Charity Independent Examiners (ACIE) (for contact details see *Useful addresses*). As well as the wide range of people from other backgrounds who are acting as independent examiners, a significant number of ACIE Full Members are qualified accountants who specialise in small and medium charities. For a charity looking to find an experienced independent examiner, ACIE can provide lists of Full Members.

Reporting accountant

For charitable companies, the requirements for scrutiny of the accounts are determined by the Companies Acts 1985 and 1989 (as amended), not by the Charities Act or Scottish rules on charity accounts. If your organisation is a charitable company and you are working with accountants who are not charity specialists you may need to draw their attention to the special provisions in the Companies Acts for companies which are charities, as the scrutiny requirements start at lower levels of income than for other companies.

In general, provided none of the company's members object, a charitable company with income in the range £90,000 to £250,000 can opt for an 'audit exemption report' by a reporting accountant, instead of a full audit. If the accounts are satisfactory, the report will say that in the opinion of the reporting accountant:

- the accounts are in agreement with the accounting records;
- the accounts are consistent with the requirements of the Companies Act;
- the company is entitled to exemption from audit.

The second point should include some checks that the Charities SORP (see chapter 2) has been followed (since the Companies Act requires companies to follow relevant accounting standards) but the duties of a reporting accountant are considerably less than for an independent examination (however, at present there is no legal provision for an independent examination of a charitable company's accounts).

Whilst independent examiners can come from many backgrounds, a reporting accountant must be a qualified accountant (a member of one of eight specified professional bodies) holding a public practising certificate and independent of the trustees/directors (but the person does not have to be a registered auditor).

Full audit

For a charity with an income of over £250,000 (£100,000 for unincorporated charities in Scotland), the accounts must be subject to a full audit by a firm of registered auditors (this is more than just being a qualified accountant – registered auditors must meet specified criteria and are subject to extensive professional monitoring).

An audit report goes further than an independent examination or reporting accountant's report; an audit report, if satisfactory, states that in the auditor's opinion the accounts give a 'true and fair view' of the charity's state of affairs and income and application of resources. (This is for accruals accounts. In the rare event of a full audit of accounts on a receipts and payments basis, the auditor declares that they are 'properly presented'.)

The precise terms of the audit are slightly different according to whether the charity is a company, but in all cases a charity audit goes a good deal further than a general audit. For example, the regulations under the Charities Act require the auditor to check whether restricted funds are properly shown. Furthermore, in saying whether the accounts give a true and fair view, the auditor has to consider the accounting standards used, including the Charities SORP.

Selecting a reporting accountant or auditor

To find a reporting accountant or auditor you will, in practice, almost always need to use a firm of accountants. The key thing is to find a firm appropriate to your size of organisation with reasonable experience with charities and voluntary organisations.

You can either start from local directories (such as Yellow Pages), ask for recommendations from other local charities, or approach the professional accountancy bodies (see *Useful addresses*) most of which offer a referral service for organisations seeking an accountant. They may also be able to give you details of charity specialists in your area.

Either way, you must normally expect to pay proper fees for accountants' time and costs. Some firms have lower rates for charities, but an audit always involves considerable expenses, and with charity accounts now forming a specialist field, free charity audits are becoming quite rare.

Some charities seeking a full audit ask two or three firms to tender, but you must be clear about what you are seeking, what information you will supply, and the timescales involved (remember many groups have a 31 March year end, so charity accountants tend to be very busy in the spring and early summer). But don't just choose the cheapest figure – look at whether the firm really has the expertise to understand your charity.

Issuing the accounts to others

Whenever you are asked to send a copy of your accounts (for example with a funding application), you must always provide:

- the annual report (signed by the trustees);
- the annual accounts (signed by the trustees);
- the independent report on the accounts (signed by the auditor, independent examiner or reporting accountant).

Once everything is complete and signed, it is worth getting enough copies made for your trustees, members, funders and others who may need to see the accounts – normally they are photocopied as a single document. A photocopied or printed signature is fine, so long as the name and date of approval are clear. Remember that, as a charity, your annual report and accounts form a public document, and anyone is entitled to see them (if necessary you can make a small charge to cover photocopying and postage).

However, the accounts should never be copied to anyone external until you have all three elements – the annual report, the accounts and the independent report – complete and signed (many funders will, quite rightly, reject unsigned accounts or accounts without the independent report, because legally they are no more than draft documents). If your accounts are not complete and you need to send accounts urgently to someone such as a prospective funder or donor, it is much better to send the previous year's accounts – perhaps with a covering letter explaining recent developments – rather than to send incomplete accounts for the current year.

9 Management accounts and budgets

As shown in chapter 2, accounts are not just a legal requirement at year end, they are vital for making day to day financial decisions in a charity. So, although the structure of your books needs to relate to the legal requirements, this is hardly their main purpose. In a well-run organisation, the largest use of information from the books is for ongoing financial monitoring and for decisions by trustees throughout the year.

Presenting information internally

Taking information from the books and presenting it in a form for internal decisions is the field of *management accounting*. Management accounting in a charity is also concerned with monitoring figures against budgets, analysing the cost-effectiveness of different approaches and handling issues of cashflow.

In a small charity, few people use the term 'management accounts' – most treasurers just talk about giving a current financial report – but the way you provide such information to the trustees has a huge effect on their ability to take meaningful decisions.

Traditionally, in many small charities you will hear something like the following exchange at trustees' meetings.

Chair:	And now we come to the treasurer's report. Joe – can you give us an update on how we are doing?
Treasurer:	Many thanks. I'm pleased to say we've got £273.29 in the current account and £1,503.50 in the deposit account, so we're doing quite well – we had over £200 in from the sponsored walk. But we've got some bills coming in next month so we mustn't get complacent – although I hear Sue has managed to get a new grant from a local trust, so that will help.
Sue:	Yes, but we need to bear in mind that the new grant is specifically for play equipment.
Chair:	Well that's very helpful, I'm sure the treasurer will make a note of that, and thank you once again, Joe, for all you do to keep our finances in such good order.

As a form of management accounting, this is almost useless. Apart from other factors, very few people can take in financial information that is just given verbally. But, more seriously, knowing how much is in the bank is only important if there are tight cashflow issues – a summary of income and expenditure, plus balances on each fund, will often communicate much more, especially if the income and expenditure is shown with actual figures compared with budgets.

Furthermore, as indicated by Sue's comment, this treasurer seems very vague about restricted funds (see chapter 3). As we have seen, fund accounting is not just an issue to sort out at year end to meet the charity accounting rules. It must be possible for the trustees to know at any time the resources available in each fund separately if they are to make proper decisions.

Using budgets

Budgets versus expenditure limits

Budgets are a vital tool in management accounting, but people use the word 'budget' in different ways:

- as an estimated income and expenditure account for next year (as in 'the budget of the charity was approved last night') – this is the way 'budget' is most often used in management accounts;
- as a target for the level of income or expenditure against a given account heading – one line within a budget statement in the first sense (as in 'our budget income from services is £3,000');
- as an agreed level of expenditure that can be incurred by the budget holder without further approval (as in 'I have been given a budget of up to £400 to spend on stationery').

So it is important to be clear with others what you mean. If the trustees approve a budget statement in the first sense it doesn't necessarily mean they are giving authority for all the expenditure shown in the budget without further discussion. Also, some people used to public sector budget controls think they have to spend to the limit of a budget before year end – this may occasionally be true with a time-limited restricted fund but normally, in a charity, avoiding unnecessary expenditure means more resources are left for future work.

Of course, as we saw in chapter 6, the trustees need to give delegated authority for the treasurer or finance officer to pay certain normal bills without individual discussion. Also, for certain costs you may want to give a senior member of staff the authority to spend up to a certain amount per year. But it is best to use a term such as 'authorised expenditure' to cover such policies. For example, the trustees may have agreed a budget statement that gives £500 as the estimated training expenditure in the coming year. But the policy on incurring training expenses might be quite different, with delegated authority for small amounts, but still needing trustees' approval to spend over £200 on any single training event.

Preparing budget statements

As we noted, a finance report at a trustees' meeting is little use if it only gives the bank balances, but even a report of actual income and expenditure doesn't tell people much unless they have some basis of comparison. You could simply make comparisons with last year, but in a fast changing organisation this is not always relevant. Comparing actual figures against budgets is usually the best tool.

So, in a well-run charity, towards the end of the financial year the treasurer or finance officer will prepare a draft budget for discussion by trustees, showing for each line of income how much the charity reasonably expects to receive next year, and for each line of expenditure, an estimate of the costs. A draft budget looks just like an income and expenditure account (or receipts and payments account), but the figures are estimates for the future, rather than actual figures from the past. Where there are several funds (see *Funds in management accounts*, page 102) a separate budget statement is needed for each fund.

Some lines on the budget will be easy to determine, for example income from a known grant or expenditure on a fixed rent. Other items can be calculated quite accurately, for example salaries linked to specific scales (but with salaries, remember to allow both for inflationary rises, and for individual staff moving to higher points on a scale, and don't forget the employer's national insurance on top). However, some income lines, such as 'fundraising', can be very hard to predict accurately in a small charity – these uncertainties need to be highlighted.

If you have inter-fund transfers, such as for management fees (see chapter 3), remember to include a line in the budget for these. The management fee is a certainly an expense of the fund or project, and it will leave other funds in deficit if the transfer isn't made. Alternatively, if all overheads are charged directly to each fund, remember to include the share of overheads in the project budget. On the other hand, a project sometimes has a specific subsidy from another fund, allowing you to show a funds transfer on the income side of the budget.

Many people think that budget statements have to balance, but there are three possibilities:

- surplus budget: planned income > planned expenditure
- deficit budget: planned income < planned expenditure
- balanced budget: planned income = planned expenditure

A surplus budget is essential if you need to build up reserves (see chapter 4). On the other hand, if a project has funds brought forward from the previous year, which are now to be spent, a deficit budget for the coming year is quite normal.

When preparing a draft budget, it is often best to put the estimates together and present the draft to the trustees for discussion, even if there is a large surplus or deficit. If the draft shows an unacceptable deficit, the trustees can then discuss what expenditure to cut, or they can resolve to increase income (thus creating a case for fundraising). If you present a draft budget that balances, they may just approve it without serious discussion.

Since a budget statement is based on estimates, you need to be clear about any assumptions used. All budget statements can be optimistic or cautious (pessimistic). An optimistic budget assumes good levels of income and modest costs; a cautious budget allows for the highest levels of expenditure that might be needed but only assumes modest income. But if you prepare a pessimistic budget to make the case for more funds, make sure everyone realises the expenditure figures are worst cases and do not represent approved levels of expenditure.

Like the accounts themselves, budgets can be prepared on an accruals or a receipts and payments basis (see chapter 2). This makes a big difference when budgeting for capital items: in an accruals-based budget the cost of capital items will be spread over several years with a provision for depreciation each year, but on the receipts and payments basis, the full cost of a capital item is shown in the budget for the year when the purchase is made, with no cost in later years.

However, when drawing up budgets for fundraising bids, many funders dislike seeing 'depreciation' and prefer to see capital costs and operating costs listed separately.

Using budgets in management accounts

If a realistic budget statement has been agreed, the best way of presenting interim financial reports is by showing actual figures against budgets, as in figure 9.1. In many cases, computer-based accounting systems allow you to enter budget figures, so they can automatically generate reports of actuals against budgets. However, do make sure the 'actuals' column adds on the balance brought forward from last year in order to show the current balance of the fund – this is vital in knowing what is actually available to spend.

Some people like to add a column for the *budget variance* – the difference between the actual figure and the budget figure. More elaborate reports are most easily produced using spreadsheets, but many computer-based systems allow you to transfer figures from the accounts to a spreadsheet precisely for this purpose.

You need to be clear about positive and negative variances: on the income side a positive variance is good; but on the expenditure side you hope for a negative variance (actual expenditure less than budget expenditure). If you have entered a non-zero budget value for every line on the report, the variance can also be presented as a percentage using the formula:

$$\text{Budget Variance (\%)} = \frac{\text{Actual} - \text{Budget}}{\text{Budget}} \times 100$$

But adding variances means more columns on reports, so do be sure your trustees will understand this – knowing that 'The budget variance on stationery is –77.5%' may actually exclude people rather than helping them.

Breaking down the income and expenditure

A key issue with budget statements is how much detail to show. For a very simple fund you might need just one income line and one expenditure line. However, for the fund representing the main work of the charity, you may need ten or more income lines and perhaps up to 30 expenditure lines.

Large organisations sometimes use multi-level budgets with different degrees of summary, but this is rarely needed in a local charity. So try to

Figure 9.1 Example of a year end budget report to trustees

MIDSHAM COMMUNITY ASSOCIATION – GENERAL FUND BUDGET REPORT
Internal Report for Trustees Only

01 Apr 00 – 31 Mar 01 £		*Budget 12 Months £*	01 Apr 01 – 31 Mar 02 £
	Receipts		
467.00	Members' Subscriptions	*500.00*	534.00
10,000.00	Council Grant	*25,000.00*	25,000.00
500.00	Miscellaneous Donations	*400.00*	429.50
0.00	Tax Reclaimed on Gift Aid	*170.00*	139.89
1,103.00	Christmas Bazaar	*1,100.00*	1,731.59
71.00	Bank Interest	*60.00*	52.96
12,141.00	TOTAL RECEIPTS	*27,230.00*	27,887.94
	Payments		
980.00	Administrator Salary	*1,200.00*	1,079.00
934.00	Heat & Light	*1,000.00*	868.88
389.00	Rates, Water Rates, Cleaning	*400.00*	402.57
321.00	Stationery	*300.00*	291.40
783.00	Publicity Literature	*1,000.00*	1,781.00
1,089.00	Postage & Telephone	*1,100.00*	1,237.03
0.00	Purchase of Minibus	*18,000.00*	18,000.00
200.00	Independent Examiner's Fee	*200.00*	200.00
171.00	Committee Travel Expenses	*200.00*	126.00
6,981.00	Repairs & Maintenance	*4,000.00*	3,708.15
0.00	Contribution to Outreach Project	*0.00*	100.00
	Contingency	*50.00*	
11,848.00	TOTAL PAYMENTS	*27,200.00*	27,794.03
293.00	SURPLUS (OR DEFICIT)	*220.00–*	93.91
80.45	Balance brought forward 01 Apr 01		373.45
373.45	Balance carried forward 31 Mar 02		467.36

NOTE:

1. This is the final report for the whole year – it is presented in the same format as the budget reports you have seen earlier.
2. The left hand column shows the figures used in our published receipts and payments account for 2000/01. The far right column shows the actual figures for the year to March 2002 (subject to any adjustments by our independent examiner). The Budget column shows the 2001/02 budget figures which we agreed in February 2001.
3. You will recall that we budgeted for a £220 deficit for the year, after allowing for the minibus purchase and the increase in the Council grant. We felt we could meet a small deficit because we expected to carry forward about £300 (actually £373.45) from 2000/01.
4. However, we have actually made a small surplus of £93.91. The main gains are due to better than expected receipts from the Christmas Bazaar; and lower than expected costs for Administrator Salary (less overtime than expected) and for Heat & Light and Repairs. But you will see that several expenditures areas were higher than predicted, particularly Publicity Literature. The final cost of the minibus was exactly as per the quotation which we used for the budget. Because of the deal we got, so far we have not incurred any running costs for the minibus, but we will need to include these in 2002/03.

Fred Smith – Treasurer 4.4.02

ensure the full budget for any fund can show income, expenditure and balances on one page (no more than two) in a normal typeface.

Remember that in order to monitor actual figures against budgets, every line will have to be maintained as a separate category in your books (see chapter 5), so the more categories you create, the more complex the bookkeeping. If you have nine funds and they all have 30 kinds of expenditure, your books will need 270 expenditure accounts (9 x 30). This is not difficult with a computer system, but great care is needed to ensure expenditure is posted correctly. Moreover, if everything is budgeted, you will then have 270 separate expenditure budgets to monitor. So try to keep things simple.

Funds in management accounts

As we are starting to see, budget reports are fairly straightforward for a single fund or project. But if a charity has nine funds – say a general fund and eight restricted funds – then the trustees are managing nine different resources. It is almost like running nine organisations. You may need to take time with new trustees to ensure they appreciate this.

You therefore really need separate management accounts for each fund. But although it is possible to produce an income and expenditure report for each fund showing actual figures against budgets, this would mean your management accounts would run to at least as many pages as the number of funds – and people simply won't read them.

Some trustees from a commercial background say 'I can't follow this – I want to see one overall budget' but it simply does not make sense to mix income and expenditure for different funds in a single budget report. Knowing that you are underspent on the salaries budget across the whole charity doesn't mean you can take on a general administrator if the underspend is mainly due to a specific unfilled post in a restricted fund.

Usually the best compromise is to provide:

- a summary report showing the financial position of the whole charity, broken down by funds (but without trying to show budgets);
- detailed income and expenditure budget reports for one or two funds where key decisions are needed (a capable treasurer will consider what is important for a given meeting).

As regards the summary for the whole charity, many organisations find that once trustees are used to the SOFA (see chapter 7) it can actually be very useful, not just at year end but also as a management report during the year. It shows immediately the split of resources between unrestricted and restricted funds, including the balances brought forward, and the income lines make it easy to distinguish what has come in through grants and donations, through trading and fees, and through investment income.

However, the SOFA lumps all the restricted funds together in one column, which means you may not easily spot an individual restricted fund that is close to being overspent. So another helpful way of presenting a summary of the whole charity is simply to show a line for each fund, as in figure 9.2.

Figure 9.2 Example of a report to trustees summarising movements on all funds

MIDSHAM COMMUNITY ASSOCIATION

SUMMARY OF MOVEMENTS ON ALL FUNDS 01 Apr 01 TO 31 Mar 02

BALANCE 01 Apr 01 £	FUND	INCOME £	EXPENSES £	TRANSFERS £	BALANCE 31 Mar 02 £
	UNRESTRICTED FUNDS				
2,313	General Fund	27,918	14,444	100–	15,687
2,313	Totals for Unrestricted Funds	27,918	14,444	100–	15,687
	RESTRICTED FUNDS				
0	Outreach Project	4,713	4,554	100	259
0	Play Equipment Fund	5,000	0	0	5,000
39	Midsham Disability Project	143	73	0	109
39	Totals for Restricted Funds	9,856	4,627	100	5,368
	CAPITAL FUNDS				
120,000	Buildings Reserve	0	0	0	120,000
120,000	Totals for Capital Funds	0	0	0	120,000
122,352	TOTALS FOR ALL FUNDS	37,774	19,071	0	141,055

Fred Smith – Treasurer 4.4.02

Charity-specific computer accounting systems are likely to have a means of generating this, because a report like this is needed as one of the notes to the accounts. This type of report also makes it easy to spot when there are still funds in hand on a project that has finished, so that appropriate decisions can be taken.

Frequency of reports and accounting periods

It is best to link your management accounts into the cycle of trustees' meetings. For example, if your accounting year starts on 1 April and the trustees would like to see quarterly reports on finances, having trustees' meetings in mid-July, mid-October, etc., may work well.

If you have monthly trustees' meetings it is worth asking whether you really need full management accounts every month, or whether bi-monthly or quarterly would suffice. Although finance is important, it is not the only issue to discuss. For a small charity, the change in the financial picture during just one month may not be significant.

Once you have established the cycle of reporting, you need to decide whether to divide the year into separate accounting periods, or whether 'year-to-date' reports will be best. For example, at the October trustees' meeting when you present figures for the second quarter (July-September) would it be best to show just the last three months' income and expenditure, or would it be more meaningful to show the year so far (April–September)?

To do separate reports for each quarter, you will need to close off your books, or select 'close of period' on your computer system at the end of each quarter. Figures for a single period are most useful with trading income, where you may need to monitor profitability for each period separately, but for general monitoring year-to-date figures can be more meaningful.

When producing reports for part of the year, you also need to decide whether to show part year budgets or full year figures. For example, at the nine month point (April–December in this case) it can be useful to see whether you are over or under budget based on 9/12 of the full year budget. Other people prefer to show the full year budget so it is clear (particularly on income) whether you are close to the full year target. A third possibility is to show just the last period (October–December) against 3/12 of the budget.

Computer-based accounting systems will often give you a huge choice of reports of this kind: it is worth experimenting with the options and then settle on one format that suits your trustees.

Also, bear in mind that some funders will need you to report on a 12-month cycle that is different from your normal accounting year: this may mean combining period figures from two different accounting years.

Cashflow

We saw in chapter 4 the importance of cashflow planning for some charities. This is quite separate from normal budgeting, but where cashflow is tight your management accounts may need to include cashflow projections.

A cashflow forecast is usually presented as a table, showing the expected money in and money out each month on a cumulative basis (this must be done on a receipts and payments basis, even if the charity is otherwise doing accruals accounts, because it is the cash in and out that matters). Alternatively, it can help to present the cashflow as a graph.

A spreadsheet can be helpful in putting together the figures, but you cannot expect to generate this automatically from an accounting system, since your books (whether manual or computerised) will only tell you about the past. Figures from the past may help your projections, but a forecast can only be prepared by someone with a good knowledge of the expected future income and expenditure streams and the timings.

When doing a cashflow forecast for a new project, the largest negative figure determines how much money you must have in hand from somewhere else to support the cashflow – for example if the forecast goes to –£10,000 at its lowest point, the charity must not undertake the work unless you can support the project with £10,000 of working cash from elsewhere (preferably more, to allow for contingencies). Also, the trustees must be satisfied that risks of the project do not jeopardise other funds.

The working cash could come from other funds of the charity, via a loan from another charity, a donor, or via a conventional bank loan (but if the charity considers borrowing, do make sure the powers in the governing document allow this – it is worth taking professional advice on such issues). Alternatively, when you demonstrate the cashflow problems, you may be able to persuade the funder to pay earlier, particularly if it is keen for you to do the work.

If cashflow is the main issue, your management accounts will want to focus on actual cash received and paid out each month compared with the projected cashflow from the project plan. Frequent trustees' meetings may be vital to monitor this closely, and if problems occur, expenditure may have to be postponed. If there is any chance that the charity may run out of funds completely, take professional advice urgently, or the trustees could find they are acting illegally.

Supporting a charity through a major cashflow crisis is perhaps one of the ultimate tests for a treasurer or finance officer.

Communicating accounts meaningfully

Producing management accounts has no value unless they are meaningful to the readers. You cannot expect trustees to make informed decisions unless they understand the information they are given.

Pure verbal reports are not much use, but neither is a large pile of papers with numerous figures and few comments. Try to get management accounts circulated before the meeting if possible. At the meeting, talk people through what you have provided (but without commenting on every figure) and encourage questions. With larger meetings, showing the figures on an overhead projector can help. It can be useful to have one trustees' meeting each year – perhaps the annual budget-setting meeting – when someone explains the overall structure of the charity's accounts and the purpose of each fund.

Try to use meaningful names for accounts and funds and other matters such as font sizes, paper colours, and other readability issues (and use a consistent format). Graphical presentations can help, particularly if trustees are being asked to decide between two options – if you are an experienced spreadsheet user this will not be difficult. If any trustees have disabilities affecting what they can read, you need to take this into account – ask them directly what they would like.

However, do bear in mind that spending hours each month or quarter reformatting your accounts in spreadsheets can add enormously to the work of the treasurer or finance officer, so be wary of taking on ever increasing demands that you cannot sustain. If the standard printouts from your computer-based accounting system can serve as management accounts, it is obviously much easier.

10 Accruals accounting

As explained in chapter 2, once a charity's total income (across all funds) exceeds £100,000, the final accounts must be prepared on an accruals basis and presented in SORP format. (In fact, many charities will want to do this at lower levels of income, either to give a more professional look to the accounts, or it may be a legal requirement if the charity is a company or is based in Scotland – see chapter 2.)

For many treasurers and finance staff, the SORP format is not the problem: once you understand the idea of fund accounting, the layout of the SOFA and balance sheet is quite logical. What often needs more thought, if you don't have a formal accounting background, is making the correct postings in the books (or on your computer system), for example for debtors, creditors and fixed assets.

Who does what?

If you feel the accruals principles are too much for you, it is possible to keep the books during the year on a receipts and payments basis, and then pay an accountant at year end to convert everything to accruals for the final accounts. Accountants are used to working on this basis, and it is probably better to use this option than to try accruals accounting with the possibility of making a number of incorrect entries.

However, if you do this, it means that your internal management accounts may end up looking very different from your final accounts. For example, you may think a fund had money in hand at year end, but once the accountant has adjusted for a creditor, the fund may be in deficit in the final accounts. On the other hand, a fund might appear fully spent when calculated on a receipts and payments basis, but once a fixed asset purchase is capitalised (see *Fixed assets,* page 112), the fund may look as though very little has been spent.

It is helpful to have at least some understanding of the accruals principles used by your accountant to make these adjustments. Otherwise you may have to ask your trustees to approve accounts you don't understand yourself. Moreover, if you send out accounts that you don't really understand, how will you deal with queries from funders?

It follows that if you can get on top of the basic principles of accruals accounting, there is a lot to be said for keeping your books on this basis in the first place if the final accounts will be accruals-based.

Standard bookkeeping texts offer much more on these concepts than we can cover in a short book (see *Further reading*). The rest of this chapter summarises the issues and give some examples.

Concepts of accruals accounts

The key principle of accruals accounts is that they show the income due to the charity (or to a certain fund) during the year and the costs and expenses incurred. This is clearly a better way of understanding the charity's resources and demands than simply recording cash in and out. For more on this and some of the differences, see *Accruals or receipts and payments?* in chapter 2.

But showing income and expenditure in terms of revenue earned and costs incurred has several important implications.

- *Accruals accounts may need estimates and judgements* – for example, choosing a depreciation policy or deciding whether to include a promised donation as a debtor. These will affect postings in the records and hence the final figures on the SOFA and balance sheet. There are no right and wrong answers: it is a matter of judgement, and depending on the judgements made, different sets of accounts could be produced for the same charity.

  However, if you were to make ludicrous judgements, your auditor or independent examiner would have to give a qualified report. In many cases the SORP gives guidance on such issues: many paragraphs are concerned with the criteria for 'recognising income' (deciding what income should be included), and for 'recognising expenses'.
- *Accruals accounts must give a 'true and fair' view*. This is always the aim when judgements and policies are made. Such judgements ultimately have to be agreed by the trustees, on the basis of trying to ensure the accounts give a true and fair view of the charity's affairs, but in most cases the trustees will be guided by the recommendations of their treasurer, finance officer or accountant.

  Accountants spend a lot of time studying the phrase 'true and fair', but for the lay person it is best to take the words at face value. For example, if your charity had incurred a bill for £10,000 just before year end, it would hardly be 'fair' to show accounts with £2,500 in hand if, in reality, you would be £7,500 in deficit once this bill was paid. Receipts and payments accounts may show a true record of money received and paid out, but they will rarely be 'fair' in the sense of this example.

- *The four fundamental accounting concepts are assumed to apply to the accounts* (unless there is a specific note to the contrary):
  1. The *going concern basis* – unless stated otherwise, accounts are prepared on the basis that the organisation has sufficient resources to continue.
  2. The *accruals basis* – income and costs appear in the accounts as they are accrued (as they are earned and incurred).
  3. *Consistency* – where judgements are made, they should be consistent each year.
  4. *Prudence* – when in doubt, accounts should never be over-optimistic.
- *The concept of 'materiality'* applies to all figures in the SOFA, balance sheet and notes. This means that you do not have to worry about where to show something if it is too small to be material to readers of the accounts. But care is needed when applying this to charities. For example, an item that is small in relation to the charity as a whole may be material in relation to a certain fund. Even a very small payment to a trustee will almost always be material.

Also, accruals accounts should take account of *all relevant published accounting standards*. Although the Charities SORP will be the most prominent standard, other more general standards are also relevant. To save small organisations referring to numerous separate standards, the main principles are brought together in the *Financial Reporting Standard for Smaller Entities* (FRSSE – see *Further reading*).

Accruals transactions

Although people sometimes imply that accruals and receipts and payments accounting are totally distinct, the vast majority of day to day transactions, such as receiving a donation or paying wages, will be entered in the same way in both systems.

Similarly, certain transfers that have no net income or expenditure to the charity will be the same with receipts and payments or accruals. These include transactions for moving money between bank accounts, drawing petty cash and most inter-fund transfers.

Where differences arise, they mainly relate to debtors, creditors and fixed assets. Even with receipts and payments accounts, you need to keep track of these items, in order to include them on the statement of assets and liabilities. But the big difference with accruals accounting is that the value of debtors, creditors and fixed assets is directly included in the balances of the funds. This can give rise to transactions that do not involve movements of money but which affect the balances of funds.

To enter these correctly, using double entry bookkeeping is strongly recommended (see chapter 5), but if you are using a computer system, you can probably make many entries without needing to understand debits and credits. However, to cover all cases, including manual books, we use the format of debits (DR) and credits (CR) in the following examples.

Money owed to the charity (debtors)

If there is an increase in the amount of money owed to a charity (the debtors' figure), for example if you suddenly hear on 5 December 2002 that someone has died and the charity is entitled to receive a £12,000 legacy, you will need to make an entry in the books to record this income, even though it may be many months before the money is physically received. The transaction to post would be:

5 Dec 2002	DR	Debtors	£12,000
	CR	Donated income	£12,000

This appears as £12,000 income to the fund. The income appears on the SOFA, balanced by the debtors' figure on the balance sheet. This is correct: the charity is legally entitled to this money, it is part of your resources and your trustees can decide how they will spend it. (But if cashflow is tight, you might want to wait until the money comes in before actually spending it.)

When the legacy is finally paid over, perhaps not until well into the next accounting year, take care not to record it as new income: you have already 'recognised' the income previously. All that happens in the new year is that the debtor is converted to money in the bank:

13 Sep 2003	CR	Debtors	£12,000
	DR	Bank	£12,000

The effect of this is that the bank balance goes up by £12,000 and the debtors' figure is reduced by £12,000. The balance of the debtors' account is now zero (assuming there are no other debtors). Since the income was recorded previously, the fund balances are unaffected.

Money owed by the charity (creditors)

Creditors are often unpaid bills at year end. For example, on 23 March 2002 you received a gas bill for £775, but this was not paid by your year end of 31 March. Clearly this was part of the expenses of running the charity in the last year and, for a true and fair view, it must be 'recognised' as an expense. You can post this by entering:

23 Mar 2002	CR	Creditors	£775
	DR	Heat/light expenses	£775
		(If the gas bill is normally apportioned between funds, there may be several debits to different expenditure accounts.)	

The balance of the relevant fund(s) has now gone down by £775 because of this expense. The expenditure appears on the SOFA, and is balanced by the creditors' figure on the balance sheet.

In the following year when you pay the bill remember that, although you are writing a cheque, this isn't new expenditure, the expenditure was included last year. You are simply transferring money out of the bank to settle a creditor. So post this as:

23 Apr 2002	DR	Creditor	£775
	CR	Bank	£775

The bank balance has gone down and, if this was the only creditor, the creditors' balance (which was negative – in credit) is now back to zero. But the fund balances are unchanged.

Prepayments and accruals

The converse can apply where money is paid out in the year before the one to which the expenditure applies. For example, you might have to pay a large deposit to hire a venue for an event next year. This is called a *prepayment* and appears as a debtor on the balance sheet.

Conversely, you will sometimes receive income in advance, for example a grant paid early but with a clear condition that it cannot be spent until next year. Although you will have the money in the bank, the charity is not yet legally entitled to it, so it is balanced by a creditor on the balance sheet. The logic is that if the charity closed down at the end of the current year, the money would have to be repaid. You are not entitled to the income until next year. Such creditors are often referred to as *deferred income* or *accruals*.

To make matters harder, prepayments and accruals sometimes have to be estimated: for example, if it has been two months since your last gas bill, then at year end you owe a certain amount for gas even though you have not yet been billed. For really precise accounting, you need to estimate these figures and post estimated accruals.

At one time accountants placed much effort in calculating and entering such adjustments. But often a lot of work can be saved by applying the principle of materiality – would it affect a reader of the accounts? If you were running a steel works, the accrued energy costs at year end could make a big difference to a company's final accounts, but for the vast majority of small to medium charities the effect of such adjustments will be too small to be material. So long as you have paid four quarterly gas bills in the year, small adjustments at the start and end of the year will have little impact on the total picture.

Posting prepayments and accruals can become complex, and if you have to enter these you may need help. But if you can avoid them, so much the better. Sometimes the only accrual that really has to be entered is a provision for the fee to the auditor or independent examiner, and if you know the amount, you can just enter this like a normal creditor.

Fixed assets

Fixed assets need some thought, but the key thing to bear in mind is that if you are buying furniture, equipment or anything with a life of several years, the cost needs to be spread over several accounting years – this is known as *depreciation.* The depreciation figure in the accounts is a measure of how much fixed assets were 'used up' in the year concerned.

For example, if you buy a £1,500 computer and you expect it to last about three years, you will probably want to show £500 of expenditure in the accounts for three successive years. On the balance sheet, the computer appears under 'Fixed assets' with a value of £1,500 when first bought, and the value goes down as the depreciation is charged: so the value will be £1,000 after the first year, £500 after the second year and £0 after the third year. (This is 'straight-line depreciation' – there are other methods.)

The SORP does not require any specific depreciation policy: it is up to the trustees to make reasonable judgements based on the expected life of assets bought, but try to avoid anything too complex or having too many different rates. However, it is normal to have a *capitalisation limit,* where purchases for less than a certain amount (typically £100 or £250) are entered in full when the purchase is made. To depreciate items costing less than the limit, even if they might last several years, will rarely be material.

For everything above the capitalisation limit, you need a *fixed asset register,* where you record the item at the time of purchase (this is also useful for insurance purposes) and then note each year's depreciation when you enter it in the books. Without this, it is almost impossible to enter depreciation correctly for something bought several years ago.

Consider a charity that buys a minibus for £18,000. The key thing to remember when you make the purchase is that, although you have written a cheque for this amount, you are simply converting money in the bank into assets of a different sort. So the entry in the books might be:

18 Jan 2002	CR	Bank	£18,000
	DR	Fixed assets – minibus	£18,000

The bank balance has gone down by £18,000 and the fixed assets have gone up by £18,000. As yet there has been no expenditure, and the fund balances are unaffected. If, for example, the minibus is funded by a special grant, the balance of the restricted fund will still show the full £18,000. The only change is that the assets of the fund now comprise a minibus instead of cash in the bank.

It is only when you enter depreciation that the fund goes down. If the minibus is to be depreciated at 25% for the first year, the depreciation at the end of that year will be:

31 Mar 2002	CR	Fixed assets – minibus	£4,500
	DR	Expenses – depreciation	£4,500

This does not affect the bank balance, but it does represent real expenditure on the SOFA. (This example assumes the common policy of charging a whole year's depreciation in the first year, regardless of how long the asset has been held.)

The depreciation expense account must be an expenditure category in the fund that is paying for the minibus. If this was a restricted fund specifically for the minibus purchase, the balance of the fund will reduce gradually over the years (rather than immediately after purchase). This is fully in accordance with the SORP, but sometimes needs explaining to those reading the accounts.

Applying the concepts – an exercise

In the light of the principles in this chapter, you may like to look back to the examples in figures 7.1 and 7.2, which show the accounts of the same charity on a receipts and payments basis and accruals basis. Taking into account the items on the statement of assets and liabilities at the start and end of the year, you might like to see if you can work from the receipts and payments accounts in figure 7.1 to get to the SOFA and balance sheet amounts in figure 7.2. Notice the differences in the fund balances.

11 Trading income and taxes

There is a widespread myth that charities are not subject to tax. In fact the situation is much more varied, as shown in table 11.1.

Table 11.1 Taxes and charity

Examples of taxes affecting charities

A No special reliefs for charities:

- Employer's national insurance
- Insurance premium tax

B Some reliefs in specific situations:

- VAT (limited concessions for charities – growing slowly)
- Business rates (more extensive concessions)

C General relief for most charitable work:

- Corporation tax (on trading*)
- Income tax (on investment income*)
- Capital gains tax (on investment gains)
- Inheritance tax (on legacies received)

* However, even these reliefs are not universal:
- Automatic exemption from corporation tax only applies to primary purpose trading by the charity itself (see chapter 4, and below)
- Charities do not pay income tax on interest, but cannot now reclaim corporation tax deducted from share dividends

Charity taxation is a complex field, and in a book of this size we can only highlight a few key issues that treasurers of smaller charities need to keep in mind. From table 11.1, it is clear that trading income is the area that most often gives rise to problems. For more guidance, see *Further reading*, and bear in mind that the rules and thresholds change slightly each year.

The nature of trading income

In chapter 4 we explained that trading income means any income to the charity from selling goods or services (as opposed to donated income and investment income). We also saw that there are two distinct types of trading income:

- *primary purpose trading* – where the goods or services provided are directly part of the charity's objects;
- *trading for fundraising purposes* – where the goods or services provided are sold simply as a means of raising funds.

Refer back to chapter 4 for more on these terms, and examples of each case.

Whenever trading income is involved, there are two tax questions to consider:

- Should the charity be charging VAT on what we are selling?
- Is the charity liable to corporation tax if the activity makes a profit?

Charities and Value Added Tax

Most businesses are VAT registered, which means that they have to charge VAT on what they sell, but they can reclaim the VAT on what they buy.

Purchases by the charity

Many people think charities can also reclaim VAT but, in most cases this is not possible because grants, donations and investment income do not count as trading income, and the ability to reclaim VAT only applies when an organisation is trading. So normally, whenever you buy anything, your charity will have to pay the supplier's price including VAT. In the books, few local charities therefore need to show VAT separately, and just enter all expenses at the total value including VAT.

Remember to bear VAT in mind when budgeting. For example if you are quoted a price of £1,200 excluding VAT for a new photocopier, and you want to apply for a grant to cover the cost, you will need a grant of £1,410. The extra £210 is to cover the 17.5% VAT you pay to the supplier, but which the supplier passes on to the government. Across the sector, charities pay hundreds of millions of pounds of tax to the government in this way.

There are a few concessions for some items supplied to charities, but they only apply in certain fields – for example press advertisements and buildings. When someone places an advertisement in a newspaper it would normally be subject to 17.5% VAT, but if the advertisement is placed by a charity, the newspaper company is allowed to charge you 0% VAT. With buildings the rules are complex, and if you are considering major building work, get professional advice on the VAT position at an early stage.

Goods and services sold by the charity

If your charity has any trading income, the charity is classed as a business for VAT purposes. In certain cases you will need to register for VAT, and charge VAT on what you sell. If this applies, you will need to separate out the VAT amounts in your books. Your trustees must apply to register for VAT if your total trading income (across all funds and projects) exceeds the VAT registration level (£54,000 in 2001/02, although the limit increases slightly each year). However, in calculating the total trading income, you can exclude sales which, if you were VAT-registered, would be VAT exempt (see below).

VAT registration is done through your local office of HM Customs & Excise. Charities that do have to register for VAT are usually *VAT partially exempt* (because the grants and donations side is non-VATable), which makes the VAT issues more complex that in a normal business.

If this is the case, you will need further guidance – beyond the scope of this book – on VAT accounting. The aim of this section is simply to help you work out if your charity is safely below the VAT threshold, in which case you can ignore VAT issues. (If a charity has some trading income, it is possible to register for VAT voluntarily, but it is only in a few cases where you would gain by doing so.)

Where an organisation is VAT registered, it must charge VAT at the appropriate rate on everything sold. In most cases this is bad news. For example, if you sell packs of Christmas cards at £4.00 each, and the charity becomes VAT-registered you would have to charge your supporters £4.70 (inc 17.5% VAT – 70p – which you would pass on to the government). Alternatively, you could keep the price at £4.00 and absorb the VAT, but selling packs at £4.00 including VAT works out as £3.40 plus 60p VAT, so you would lose 60p on each pack sold. A charity raising thousands of pounds through Christmas cards would be much worse off.

On the other hand, if you were providing a service to your local authority, or to a normal VAT-registered business, they would not mind if you had to add VAT, because they can reclaim it. So the implications of VAT depend on your customer.

There are currently five rates or categories of VAT.

- Most goods and services are subject to *standard rate VAT* (currently 17.5%) – this includes everything not in the categories below.
- A few items are subject to a *lower VAT rate* (5%) – home energy and certain insulation and sanitary protection products.
- Some items *zero-rated for VAT* – VAT is charged as normal, but the rate is 0%. Products include books and other publications, children's clothing and cold food. VAT can still be reclaimed on purchases (for example, the paper to print the books, and so charities selling publications can often benefit from this). The 0% rate also applies to sales of donated goods (for example jumble sales and charity shops).
- Some sales are *VAT-exempt*, which means that you do not have to charge VAT on the sale but you cannot reclaim any corresponding VAT on purchases. VAT-exempt sales do not count towards the turnover in deciding whether you should be VAT registered. A number of charity services fall into this category including educational services and welfare services provided by a 'relevant' charity (see VAT publications in *Further reading* for definitions). Fundraising events exempt from corporation tax are also classed as VAT exempt (see *Charities and corporation tax*, page 119).
- Some income is classed as non-business income and is therefore *outside the scope of VAT*. This includes grants, donations and investment income.

The above list is only a very general summary – the full lists of zero-rated and VAT-exempt items take up many pages of legislation.

Should our charity be VAT registered?

If your charity's total income is more than £54,000, work out how much of this is trading income. This means being very clear whether funding agreements are grants or contracts (see chapter 4). Then deduct items that would be VAT exempt (see above). If the total comes to more than about £50,000 you will need to watch the position carefully. If it goes over the threshold you must register for VAT within a month.

Note that *all* trading income – both primary purpose trading and trading for fundraising – counts for the VAT threshold.

Here are four examples.

- Charity A has a total income of £51,000. This is below the VAT threshold, so however the income is made up, it *does not* have to register.
- Charity B has a total income of £120,000, but £75,000 of this is grants and donations. The remaining £45,000 is below the VAT threshold, so even if all of this was potentially VATable, it is below the threshold so it *does not* have to register.
- Charity C is an educational organisation. Its total income is £90,000, of which £80,000 comes from course fees. Although this is trading income above the VAT threshold, the course fees would be VAT exempt, so it *does not* have to register.
- Charity D has a total income of £100,000, £30,000 of which is from grants, donations and investments. The other £70,000 is trading income – half from publications sales and half from contracts for advice and consultancy services. All of the trading income is VATable (either at 0% or 17.5%) and as it totals more than £54,000, it *must register* immediately.

Charities and corporation tax

Corporation tax is a tax on the trading profits of companies and other business organisations (this includes charities). For any trading activity you have to work out the profit, using the rule:

Sales – Expenses = Profit

Even though the profit is only a surplus to be retained by the charity, in some cases it is subject to tax; otherwise charities would be able to run large commercial businesses on a tax-free basis, competing unfairly with other firms. Corporation tax is charged at 10%, 20% or 30% depending on the total profit. In working out the profit you can only deduct the expenses of the activity concerned (not the expenses of the whole charity), although you can include an element for the cost of voluntary time.

So, for example, a charity that runs a successful coffee shop with relatively few expenses could find that, as well as having to charge VAT, nearly 20% of its income might have to be set aside for corporation tax. But there are ways round this – described below.

Charity exemptions from corporation tax

The corporation tax rules contain a large number of charity exemptions. They are all subject to the condition that any profit is retained by the charity for the development of the service – but in a charity, the trustees could not in any case benefit from a profit.

1 *Primary purpose trading*. Where the goods or services are provided directly as part of the charity's objects, there is no liability to corporation tax (though bear in mind that VAT could still apply). This is a very important rule. Some charities waste huge effort in setting up trading subsidiary companies when the activity they want to carry out is part of the charity's central task.

   The liability to corporation tax only arises with trading for fundraising purposes. But even this has many exemptions, as summarised in the following points.

2 *Where the trade is carried out mainly by the beneficiaries of the charity* – for example workshops run by blind people, coffee shops run mainly by people with learning disabilities or a car wash service run by young people – there is no corporation tax on any profit, provided those doing the bulk of the work are the people the charity exists to support.

3 *Trades that are ancillary to the primary purpose* – for example accommodation for students or refreshments in an art gallery – these are also exempt from corporation tax.

4 *Any small scale trading and fundraising activities within set limits* are also exempt. This new rule, introduced in April 2000, is very flexible as, within limits, it exempts any kind of trading for fundraising purposes from corporation tax. The vast majority of fundraising projects by small charities will fit this, even where the activity involves selling something. The condition is that the charity's total income (not profit) from such activities is below:
   - £5000 or
   - 25% of the charity's total income, up to a maximum of £50,000 (for a charity with over £200,000 income in total).

Table 11.2 gives examples.

Table 11.2 Small scale trading for fundraising – exemption from corporation tax

Charity's total income	Maximum trading income for fundraising that can escape corporation tax	
£3,000	£3,000	(Up to £5,000 allowed anyway)
£12,000	£5,000	(£5,000 allowed anyway)
£30,000	£7,500	(25% of income)
£160,000	£40,000	(25% of income)
£250,000	£50,000	(£50,000 upper limit)

But even when the trade is beyond those limits, there are further exemptions for certain types of trading income.

5 *Sales of donated goods* (for example jumble sales, charity shops, auctions of donated gifts) are exempt from corporation tax (and for VAT the 0% rate applies).

6 There are also exemptions from corporation tax for *other specific fundraising events* (provided they are supported because people know the event is for charity) in the cases of:
   - small events of any kind, provided the takings do not exceed £1,000 per week;
   - larger events, provided the charity holds no more than 15 events per year in any venue.

   The income from such activities counts as VAT exempt.

Trading outside the concessions – trading subsidiary companies

For most smaller charities, one or more of the above concessions will almost certainly cover your fundraising activities, and a liability to corporation tax is thus quite rare. But if you do go beyond these limits, it is up to the charity to make a corporation tax return to the Inland Revenue.

However, where a charity would end up paying a lot of corporation tax, a further solution is to set up a non-charitable trading subsidiary company. For example a charity that raised funds through Christmas cards and catalogue sales could arrange for the scheme to be run by the subsidiary company rather than the charity itself. Although the company is liable to corporation tax on the profit, if it gives the whole of its profit back to the charity as a Gift Aid donation (see chapter 12), no corporation tax is paid.

Of course this means a lot of extra work – the trading subsidiary is a legally separate organisation so it needs separate accounts – and because it is not a charity it will have to pay normal business rates if it has premises. Most large charities have a trading subsidiary, but since the concessions introduced in 2000, there are now very few cases where they are needed by smaller charities.

12 Linking fundraising and accounting

As this book has stressed throughout, the overall management of a charity's finances is a matter for the trustees as a whole. But the implementation of the trustees' financial decisions normally fall to two key people or teams:

- the treasurer, together with the bookkeeper or finance officer; and
- the charity's main fundraiser (a trustee or a member of staff).

You may not use the term 'fundraiser', but there must always be someone who takes the lead on submitting grant applications, asking for donations, bidding for contracts or marketing the charity's services. Even if your charity is fortunate enough to have a regular stream of income from investments, those investments must be managed.

An accounting/fundraising team

Some charities also expect the treasurer to handle everything to do with fundraising – just because it relates to money. But this is normally too much for one person, and it is better to find ways of sharing responsibility.

Yet sadly in many charities – even in very small groups – there is often too little communication between the fundraiser and the person who handles the accounts – sometimes with disastrous results. This can be partly a matter of personality – fundraisers are often exuberant people who like to grasp opportunities and are often networking outside the confines of the charity, but they tend to find accounts rather boring. Treasurers and bookkeepers often have a quieter approach, with an emphasis on detail, and despair of getting others to follow clear procedures.

But unless a charity is successful in generating income, there will be no funds for which the treasurer has to account. On the other hand, fundraisers desperately need the charity to have good accounting procedures, so that once funds are received they are properly managed and used. There is nothing worse for a fundraiser than finding a donor or funder who makes a gift or grant but who, when approached again, is reluctant to help because they were unhappy at how the first gift was accounted for.

Here is a possible checklist of areas where you need to work out effective communication and division of responsibilities.

- *Issuing receipts for gifts* – who is responsible? Who writes the acknowledgement letter? With a large-scale appeal, the response handling and accounting for gifts may well be the biggest task.
- *Purpose of gifts* – is there a simple mechanism to ensure the treasurer or bookkeeper knows which fund every grant or donation relates to?
- *New restricted funds* – is the fundraiser authorised to invent new projects (would mean new restricted funds) or must this be approved by others? How does the treasurer or bookkeeper know when to create a new fund in the books?
- *Costing of new projects* – when bidding for funds, who works out what to ask for? And if you don't get all you ask for, who decides whether to continue or whether to drop the project?
- *Deciding when to refuse a gift.*
- *Pledges verses actual gifts* – once you have a promise of support, who is responsible for contacting the donor or funder to ensure the gifts are received? Sometimes a fundraiser feels an appeal is complete when the target is reached. But it may need four or five years of accounting for regular donations (and issuing reminders where needed) before all the funds are in the bank.
- *Banking of income* – who does what, especially with fundraising events? Is the treasurer expected to have people calling unexpectedly with bags of cash? Or are those who organise cash collections responsible for counting and banking the proceeds? (Remember the need for controls – see chapter 6.)
- *Showing income on the SOFA* – when money comes in from fundraising events, are the trading and donated income distinguished? If not, how can you get a sensible estimate of the split?
- *Cash floats* – if you are running a stall of any kind, what is the procedure for drawing and accounting for cash floats?
- *Fundraising expenses* – fundraisers need to keep a note of the costs of fundraising activities run by the charity so they can be included

correctly in the accounts. Under the SORP, you cannot just show the net income.

- *Paying advance fundraising costs* – if a fundraising activity needs payment up front, for example to hire a venue or print brochures, who approves this? What about cashflow (see chapter 9)?
- *Gift Aid tax claims* – if you have donations from individuals, it will usually be possible to reclaim tax under Gift Aid (see *Gift Aid*, below). Who will manage this? Who is responsible for getting Gift Aid declarations completed? Who actually signs the tax claim submitted to the Inland Revenue? And if the claim covers gifts for different funds, do you know how to split the tax recovered?
- *Fundraising database* – if you have more than about 20 donors you will probably need a donor database of some kind, to keep track of who has given what, and this will probably link to the Gift Aid procedures. Who is responsible for this? If the fundraiser, is he or she aware of the need for auditability of the information (by both the charity's auditor/independent examiner and by the Inland Revenue)?
- *Incoming standing orders* – if you have donors making regular gifts by bankers order, who checks the bank statement against the donor's pledges? (It is generally best if the statement first goes to the person who records gifts into the fundraising database, and then to the treasurer with a total for the main books. If this is cumbersome, consider having a separate bank account for incoming standing orders.)
- *Credit/debit card gifts* – more local charities are starting to accept these – who is responsible for the procedures?
- *CAF and similar cheques* – the Charities Aid Foundation (CAF) has schemes where donors pay into a CAF account on which tax is reclaimed, and the donors can direct funds to any charity of their choice by writing a CAF cheque. But once received by the charity, the cheques must be sent off to CAF, who will pay the funds into your bank. Who handles this? Do you have a means to ensure such gifts are not erroneously treated as Gift Aid? (Some other agency charities have similar schemes.)
- *Funders requiring invoices* – the charity will have to invoice the funder for work done under contract – who is responsible? If the amount varies, who is responsible for the invoice figure? Are you clear on the

VAT issues (see chapter 11)? If invoices are raised by someone other than the treasurer, is the treasurer told to include the funder as a debtor if the amount remains unpaid at year end?

- *Subsidiary groups* – how do all these procedures work if the charity has subsidiary groups managing their own books (see chapter 6)? This is especially important with semi-independent fundraising teams – if their events are run on behalf of the charity both their income and their expenses must appear in the charity's accounts. Or are they independent groups that raise funds and simply pass them on to you as donations?

There are few charities where fewer than four or five of these issues apply. If you have established a good relationship, with plenty of communication, between yourself and those who bring in the funds, it will make your job much easier and will greatly improve the overall financial management of the charity.

The rest of this chapter addresses some of the above areas.

Gift Aid

Gift Aid is the government scheme whereby when a UK tax payer gives to charity, the charity can reclaim the income tax paid by the donor on his or her gift.

Some charities get much of their income through Gift Aid donations, and thus receive a great deal of government support for their work. The big attraction is that Gift Aid applies to any organisation with charitable status.

Regardless of the donor's personal tax rate, the gift is treated as being made net of basic rate income tax. So to work out how much tax you can reclaim, you have to *gross up* the gift. With income tax at 22%, this means you get an extra 28.2% on all donations made under Gift Aid. For example:

- Sue Brown earns £100. Assuming she pays tax at 22% basic rate, £22 tax is deducted and she will receive £78 after tax.
- If she gives the £78 to charity, and completes a Gift Aid declaration, the charity can reclaim the £22 tax she has paid. So in total, the charity gets £100.
- By completing a Gift Aid declaration, Sue has enabled the charity to gain £22 tax on top of her £78 gift. As £22 represents 28.2% of £78, the value of her gift is increased by more than 28%.

The conditions to reclaim tax are shown below.

Conditions for a reclaiming tax on a donation (Gift Aid scheme)

1 It must be a genuine donation from an identifiable individual donor
   - Not a payment for goods or services
   - Not a company donation.

2 The recipient must be a charity in UK law (this includes exempt or excepted charities).

3 Payment must actually be made and evidence of this must be available (i.e. an audit trail of money received).

4 The donor must be a UK taxpayer (income tax or capital gains tax).
   - The donor must pay enough tax in total to cover the tax being reclaimed by the charity (but tax rates do not matter).

5 The donor must make a *declaration* that he/she wishes the gift to be treated as Gift Aid.
   - The Gift Aid Declaration must cover all issues required by the regulations – but it can be open-ended to cover all future gifts. You do not have to use specific forms, and with the required procedures you can also accept declarations by telephone and e-mail.

6 The donor must not get any but the most trivial benefit from the gift – i.e. it must be a genuine donation (there are rules on maximum benefits).

7 The charity must publish annual accounts and make them available to the Inland Revenue [and anyone else] on request.

8 The charity must be willing to have its books and records for Gift Aid donations subject to Revenue Audit.

In the past, such schemes depended on large lump sums, or four year commitments under a deed of covenant, but all that was replaced in April 2000.

Once you have set up a Gift Aid scheme, it is worth including even quite small donations because it adds very little extra work, and with regular gifts the amounts build up. If someone gives £5 a month, this is £60 a year, and you will reclaim £16.92 in tax. With sixty supporters giving at this level, you will add £1,000 a year in tax reclaims. You can apply Gift Aid to membership subscriptions, provided the subscription is largely a donation, where any benefits to the member have little financial value. (But Gift Aid only applies to identified donors – not to loose cash in collecting tins and plates.)

You need to take care, however, to ensure Gift Aid Declarations are properly worded to reflect the rules, as set out in the Inland Revenue guidance (see figure 12.1). Many charities have launched appeals with donation forms where the Gift Aid declaration is invalid. You do not need to use the exact form of words shown in the figure, nor do you have to give all the options and notes, but inclusion of note 2 (or words to that effect) is a legal requirement.

Figure 12.1 Sample Gift Aid declaration

Name of charity ....

Details of donor

Title .... Forename(s) .... Surname ....
Address ....
....
.... Postcode ....

I want the charity to treat

* the enclosed donation of £ ....
* the donation (s) of £ .... which I made on ..../......../.........
* all donations I have made since 6 April 2000, and all donations I make from the date of this declaration until I notify you otherwise

as Gift Aid donations

** delete as appropriate*

Date ...../...../.....

Notes

1. You can cancel this declaration at any time by notifying the charity.
2. You must pay an amount of income tax and/or capital gains tax at least equal to the tax the charity reclaims on your donations in the tax year (currently 28p for each £1 you give).
3. If in the future your circumstances change and you no longer pay tax on your income and capital gains equal to the tax that the charity reclaims, you can cancel you declaration (see note 1).
4. If you pay tax at the higher rate you can claim further tax relief in your Self Assessment tax return.
5. If you are unsure whether your donations qualify for Gift Aid tax relief, ask the charity or ask your local tax office for leaflet IR113 Gift Aid.
6. Please notify your charity if you change your name or address.

Source: Inland Revenue Guidance Notes for Charities, 2000

Good systems and procedures are vital. You need someone methodical in charge of the scheme (and with a good respect for donor confidentiality). Special purpose computer systems are available to help with this – often linked with other fundraising facilities to help communication with supporters – and the system can then generate tax claims on the basis of gifts recorded (an example is shown below).

Provided you are claiming at least £100, you can make claims as often as you wish. The Inland Revenue normally pays tax claims as submitted, but retains the right to inspect your books, and if problems are found on a Revenue audit the charity could have to repay large amounts of tax reclaimed. It is also crucial to ensure Gift Aid Declarations are well stored. People often remain loyal to charities for decades, and a Declaration completed in 2001 could still be needed in 2050.

Figure 12.2 Example of a Gift Aid tax claim to the Inland Revenue

MIDSHAM COMMUNITY ASSOCIATION – GIFT AID TAX CLAIM 13 Jul 01

SCHEDULE OF NEW GIFT AID DONATIONS BY UK INDIVIDUALS
Reference: X999999Y

TAX YEAR 01/02 R68(New Gift Aid)(Substitute) Amounts in £

NAME OF DONOR	DATE OF LAST DONATION	AMOUNTS GIVEN	Reference
PETER BLOGGS	18 May 01	40.00	DR 1
HUGH BONE	27 Apr 01	400.00	DR 12
JANE BROWN	27 Apr 01	100.00	DR 8
JOANNA JENKINS	27 Apr 01	25.00	DR 11
SUSANNAH JONES	18 May 01	7.00	DR 2
PHILIP THOMSON-GILES	18 May 01	45.00	DR 13
ROWENA WHITELY	18 May 01	10.00	DR 10
DONOR RECORDS: 7	TOTAL GIVEN:	627.00	
	TAX RECLAIMABLE:	176.85	at 22.00%

Source: Report generated by the Kubernesis Giving and Fundraising Suite

For a small charity, such schedules can also be completed by hand, on Inland Revenue form R68(New Gift Aid). In either case, the total is then transferred to the R68(2000) claim form and signed on behalf of the charity.

If your charity hasn't previously operated Gift Aid, contact the Inland Revenue (Charities) section for guidance notes (see *Useful addresses*), who will allocate you a reference number (distinct from your registered charity number), which must be shown on all claims.

Gift Aid means that any charity that can generate gifts from individuals can get further help from the government. But to operate it effectively needs careful co-ordination between fundraisers and treasurers.

Costing projects and fundraising bids, and refusing gifts

Not all offers of money are helpful to a charity. Donations subject to very tight restrictions may be simply too much work to justify a restricted fund for one specific gift. Also, some restrictions might break your own policies or even be illegal. For example, few charities would feel it right to accept gifts with conditions on the race of beneficiaries, unless it was a project addressing specific racial disadvantage.

But just as damaging are offers of funds that require the charity to do something, but don't cover the full costs, including relevant overheads and management time. Sometimes the trustees will feel the project is sufficiently central to their objects to justify subsidising it with a contribution from general funds. But very often treasurers find out too late that someone has committed the charity to a new project that had not been properly costed, and which will prove a net drain on the charity's general funds.

Issues of costing and budgeting have been addressed in several chapters. The time to work out costs is when a new project is first being considered, and this needs close liaison between the fundraiser and treasurer or finance officer to ensure everything is included. It is all too easy to forget the VAT, the professional fees, the employer's national insurance, the cost of salary increments over the life of the project, the recruitment costs, the premises overheads, the maintenance costs of capital items, the increase in accountancy costs, the management time to supervise a project, and all the other elements involved.

If you tell a funder, 'We need £40,000 to do this', you may get what you ask for. Even if you don't, you have only lost the cost of the time spent on the proposal. But if you say you can do it for £30,000, get the go ahead, and then come back asking for more money, most funders are likely to refuse and will also regard the charity as less than competent when it comes to future requests. The lower bid may succeed, but at a net cost to the charity of £10,000. If the funder could really only find £30,000 it might be better to refuse to do the project (or to propose something smaller where £30,000 would cover everything).

Charity finance as a whole

In this book we have looked at a vast range of financial issues, from basic bookkeeping to the legal requirements for charity accounts, to issues of charity tax, and implications for fundraising. You will have seen how these issues need to be considered as a whole, and the idea that a treasurer or finance officer is just someone who 'keeps the books' does not make any sense, even in the smallest charity.

In order to make this a 'handbook' that can be read in a few hours, there are many topics only mentioned in passing, and if such issues affect your charity, you will need to refer to further sources or seek professional guidance. Also, the field of charity finance is constantly developing. But if you have a general understanding of the topics covered here, you will be very well placed to support your charity in its management of finance.

Being an effective charity treasurer or finance officer is partly about good accounting procedures, and partly about understanding the legal requirements, so that you can advise and support your trustees. But it is also about recognising the privilege of managing monies that are not your own, which have been given to your charity in the hope of making the world a better place. If, by taking on the finance role, you can enable your charity's funds to be used effectively for the cause set out in its objects, you will be making a major contribution to society.

Further reading

Charity Commission publications

The Charity Commission produces a wide range of guidance booklets for charities. In almost all cases they apply to excepted charities as well as registered charities, and although aimed at charities in England and Wales, most are also useful for charities in Scotland and Northern Ireland. (See *Useful addresses* for contact information – the publications are also available on the Commission's website.) The following are particularly relevant to treasurers and finance workers.

CC8 – *Internal Financial Controls for Charities*

CC19 – *Charities' Reserves*

CC35 – *Charities and Trading*

CC57 – *Receipts and Payments Accounts Pack*

CC58 – *Accruals Accounts Pack*

CC60 – *The Hallmarks of a Well-Run Charity*

CC61– *Charity Accounts 2001 – The Framework*

CC63 – *Independent Examination of Charity Accounts 2001*

CC66 – *SORP 2000: Example Report and Accounts* – Note that these examples are all large charities

Accounting and Reporting by Charities: Statement of Recommended Practice October 2000 (the 2000 SORP)

Any treasurer of a charity whose income is over £100,000 should certainly have a copy of the full SORP. For smaller charities, CC57 or CC58 packs will be useful.

Books on preparing published charity accounts

Some of these were originally issued for the 1995 rules but, in several cases, new editions are now appearing to cover the 2000 rules.

Charity Accounts: A Practical Guide to the Charities SORP, Andrew Pianca, Jordans, 2002, £35

Charity Finance Accounts Compliance Checklist, Don Bawtree, Charity Finance Magazine/Plaza Publishing, 2001, £45

Clubs and Associations: An Industry Accounting and Auditing Guide, Valerie Steward, Accountancy Books, 1999, £65
Covers the framework for organisations constituted as industrial and provident societies

The ICSA Guide to Charity Accounting, Adrian Randall, ICSA Publishing, 2001, £14.95

A Practical Guide to Accounting by Charities, Kate Sayer, Directory of Social Change, 1996, £12.95

Preparing Charity Accounts, Adrian Randall, Anthony Epton and Fiona Young, Accountancy Books, 2001, £60

Legislation on charity accounts

Charities Act 1993, HMSO
Part VI of the Act covers the accounting requirements. However, the Act was amended by the Deregulation and Contracting Out Act, and a copy of Part VI as amended is needed – this is included in the *Core Guide* – see below.

Charities (Accounts and Reports) Regulations 1995 (SI 1995/2724), HMSO
These Regulations are still in force as regards the duties of auditors and independent examiners (Regs 6, 7 and definitions) – but those parts dealing with charity accounts and annual reports and have been superseded by the 2000 Regulations.

Charities Accounts and Reports Core Guide, HMSO, 1995
Includes Part VI of the Charities Act 1993 as amended, the 1995 Regulations (as above) and comments on the whole regime. However, note that the framework is changed by 2000 Regulations; see below.

Charities (Accounts and Reports) Regulations 2000 (SI 2000/2868), HMSO
These are the current Regulations on the contents of charity annual reports, and for charity accounts prepared on an accruals basis. They refer extensively to the SORP, so you need a copy of the SORP to apply them. (For receipts and payments accounts, the only requirement in law is s42(3) of the Charities Act 1993 plus the audit/independent examination rules in the 1995 Regulations.)

There are also many guidance documents issued by umbrella organisations, and some are compulsory if the charity is to retain the recognition of the body to which it belongs. For example, Church of England PCCs must comply with the Church Accounting Regulations 1997, details of which are explained in *The Charities Act 1993 and the PCC* (Church House Publishing). But it is important to note that such sector-specific rules can only supplement the general rules applicable to all charities.

Charities Accounts (Scotland) Regulations 1992 (SI 1992/2165), HMSO

Financial Reporting Standard for Smaller Entities (FRSSE), Accounting Standards Board
A general standard for financial reporting – with guidance on general accounting policies; broader issues than the charity-specific addressed by the SORP.

Books on charity financial management

Accounting and Finance for Charities: For Love and Money, David Wise, ICSA Publishing/Prentice Hall, 1998, £14.95

Charity Investigations, Andrew Burgess, Tolley Publishing, 2001, £38.95
Explains how a charity should deal with an audit visit or investigation by, for example, the Charity Commission, Inland Revenue (Charities), Inland Revenue (Employers) or Customs & Excise

The Good Financial Management Guide, Haroon Bashir, NCVO Publications, 1999, £18

The Good Financial Management Training Manual, Paul Palmer, NCVO Publications, 2001, £20
Includes useful examples on costing projects, apportioning overheads, and similar issues

A Practical Guide to Financial Management for Charities, Kate Sayer, Directory of Social Change, 1998, £14.95

Charities and tax issues

Charity Taxation: A Definitive Handbook, Adrian Randall and Stephen Williams, Jordans, 2001, £35

The Donations to Charity by Individuals (Appropriate Declarations) Regulations 2000 (SI 2000/2074), HMSO
The official regulations for Gift Aid declarations

Inland Revenue Guidance Notes for Charities, Inland Revenue
Explains the rules for operating Gift Aid and covers other charity tax issues handled by the Inland Revenue

A Practical Guide to PAYE for Charities Kate Sayer, Directory of Social Change, 1995, £9.95

A Practical Guide to VAT for Charities and Voluntary Organisations, Kate Sayer, Directory of Social Change, 2001, £12.95

Value Added Tax – Charities, HM Customs & Excise VAT Notice 701/1
Summarises the main VAT rules specific to charities, through various supplementary notices may also be applicable

Bookkeeping and accounting in general

There is a wide range of introductory books on accounting and bookkeeping in general, which clearly explain issues such as double entry bookkeeping, methods of depreciation, cashflow forecasting, and similar issues. The following are examples – most are aimed at students of bookkeeping or accounting. However, most books base their examples on commercial traders, and do not therefore cover charity-specific issues in any detail.

Accounting Theory and Practice, M W E Glautier and B Underdown, Pearson Education, 2000, £31.99

Book-keeping, Andrew Piper and Andrew Lymer, Teach Yourself Books, 1998, £8.99

Elements of Accounting, Philip Cahill, McGraw Hill, 1998, £28.99

Broader issues of charity law

Charitable Status, Andrew Phillips, Directory of Social Change, forthcoming 2002, c. £9.95

Charity Law A–Z: Key Questions Answered, John Claricoat and Hilary Phillips, Jordans, 1998, £19.50

The Charity Trustee's Handbook, Mike Eastwood, Directory of Social Change, 2001, £7.95

The Voluntary Sector Legal Handbook, Sandy Adirondack and James Sinclair Taylor, Directory of Social Change, 2001, £42

Periodicals

Charity Finance, Plaza Publishing, Editor Heather Lamont
The main specialist journal for professionals in the charity finance field

Charity Finance Yearbook, Charity Finance/Plaza Publishing
Published annually, this contains an excellent range of up to date articles and useful addresses

Independent Examiner, Association of Charity Independent Examiners, Editor Gareth G Morgan
Aimed at independent examiners, but also covers a range of issues on accounting in smaller charities

Most of the general periodicals aimed at the sector include regular articles on issues of financial management, and their other articles can be very useful in enabling treasurers and finance staff to keep in touch with more general developments. The following may be useful.

Charity Times, Perspective Publishing

Third Force News, SCVO

Third Sector, Arts Publishing International

Voluntary Sector, NCVO

Voluntary Voice, London Voluntary Service Council

Useful addresses

Charity Commission

London office
Harmsworth House, 13–15 Bouverie Street, London EC4Y 8DP

Liverpool office
2nd floor, 20 Kings Parade, Queens Dock, Liverpool L3 4DQ

Taunton office
Woodfield House, Tangier, Taunton, Somerset TA1 4BL

Enquiry line: 0870 333 0123
Website: www.charity-commission.gov.uk

Inland Revenue (Charities)

For charities in England, Wales or Northern Ireland
Inland Revenue Charities, St John's House, Merton Road, Bootle, Merseyside L69 9BB
Enquiry line: 0151 472 6036/7

For charities in Scotland
Inland Revenue Charities, Meldrum House, 15 Drumsheugh Gardens, Edinburgh EH3 7UG

Enquiry line: 0131 777 4040
Website: www.inlandrevenue.gov.uk

CharityScotland

At the time of going to press, proposals for establishing CharityScotland had been made by the Scottish Charity Law Review Commission (the McFadden Commission) but had not yet been enacted by the Scottish Parliament. In the meantime, Scottish charities should continue to deal with the Inland Revenue (Charities) in Edinburgh. The address of the Commission is:

Scottish Charity Law Review Commission, Spur V1 Saughton House, Broomhouse Drive, Edinburgh EH11 2XD

HM Customs & Excise

HM Customs & Excise (VAT Service)
National Advice Line: 0845 010 9000
Includes initial enquiries from organisations needing to register for VAT and requests for publications
Website: www.hmce.gov.uk

General help and advice

Directory of Social Change, 24 Stephenson Way, London NW1 2DP
Website: www.dsc.org.uk
Publications tel: 020 7209 5151; fax: 020 7391 4804; e-mail: info@dsc.org.uk
Courses and conferences tel: 020 7209 4949; fax: 020 7391 4808; e-mail: training@dsc.org.uk

Northern office: Federation House, Hope Street, Liverpool L1 9BW
Tel: 0151 708 0117 (courses and conferences)/0151 708 0136 (research); fax: 0151 708 0139; e-mail: north@dsc.org.uk

The Directory of Social Change is an independent voice for positive social change, set up in 1975 to help voluntary organisations become more effective. We do this by providing practical, challenging and affordable information and training to meet the current, emerging and future needs of the sector. Our main activities include researching and publishing reference guides and handbooks, providing practical training courses, and running conferences and briefing sessions.

We also organise Charityfair, the largest annual event for the UK voluntary sector, which offers the most extensive selection of training, advice and debate to be found under one roof. It is an excellent place for people on a tight budget to get training. Charityfair is normally held in March or April every year. For details telephone 020 7209 4949.

Voluntary sector umbrella bodies

England

National Council for Voluntary Organisations (NCVO), Regent's Wharf, 8 All Saints Street, London N1 9RL
Helpline: 0800 2 798 798

The NCVO helpline can assist any charity/voluntary organisation or trustee (you do not have to be an NCVO member) with a wide range of queries and produces a range of fact sheets – including several on charity accounting issues and details of specialist software.
Website: www.ncvo-vol.org.uk

National Association of Councils for Voluntary Service, 3rd floor, 177 Arundel Street, Sheffield S1 2NU
Tel: 0114 278 6636
Website: www.nacvs.org.uk

Almost every district in England has a council for voluntary service (CVS) (or equivalent), which can offer a wide range of practical help and advice to local voluntary and community organisations. Often this includes help on managing finances and accounts; some CVS also provide payroll services or community accounting services. NACVS can give details of your local CVS.

Charities Aid Foundation (CAF), Kings Hill, West Malling, Kent ME19 4TA
Tel: 01732 520000
Website: www.CAFonline.org

Scotland

Scottish Council for Voluntary Organisations (SCVO), 18/19 Claremont Crescent, Edinburgh EH7 4QD
Tel: 0131 556 3882
Website: www.scvo.org.uk

Wales

Wales Council for Voluntary Action (WCVA), Baltic House, Mount Stuart Square, Cardiff CF10 5FH
Enquiry line: 029 2043 1700
Website: www.wcva.org.uk

Northern Ireland

Northern Ireland Council for Voluntary Action (NICVA), 61 Duncairn Gardens, Belfast BT15 2GB
Charity Advice Service: 028 9087 7777
Website: www.nicva.org

Professional bodies concerned with charity finance

Association of Charity Independent Examiners
36 Acomb Wood Drive, York YO24 2XN
Tel: 01904 788885
Website: www.acie.org.uk

Provides support, training and a qualification for independent examiners, and a referral service for charities seeking an independent examiner.

Charity Finance Directors' Group
Camelford House, 89 Albert Embankment, London SE1 7TP
Tel: 020 7793 1400
Website: www.cfdg.org.uk

Mainly for finance directors of larger charities, but finance officers of smaller charities can also apply to join.

Institute of Charity Fundraising Managers
Market Towers, 1 Nine Elms Lane, London SW8 5NQ
Tel: 020 7627 3436
Website: www.icfm.org.uk

Although ICFM members are normally fundraisers rather than treasurers and finance staff, some of the specialist ICFM groups – for example on tax-effective giving – are also of relevance to treasurers.

Groups for specific types of charities

There are also a number of networks and associations of treasurers or finance staff within particular types of charities. If your local charity is part of a national network, contact the central office to find out if there is any specific support for local treasurers.

Other professional bodies

Many more general professional bodies have a charity-specialist group, including the ICAEW, ACCA and ICSA (see below). Registered auditors will almost always belong to ICAEW, ACCA, ICAS or ICAI. Reporting accountants may also be drawn from AAT members.

Association of Accounting Technicians (AAT)
154 Clerkenwell Road, London EC1R 5AD
Tel: 020 7837 8600
Website: www.aat.co.uk

Chartered Association of Certified Accountants (ACCA)
29 Lincoln's Inn Fields, London WC2A 3EE
Tel: 020 7242 6855
website: www.acca.co.uk

Institute of Chartered Accountants in England and Wales (ICAEW)
PO Box 433, Chartered Accountants Hall, Moorgate Place, London EC2P 2BJ
Tel: 020 7920 8100
Website: www.icaew.co.uk

Institute of Chartered Accountants in Ireland (ICAI)
Chartered Accountants House, 87–89 Pembroke Road, Ballsbridge, Dublin 4
Tel (from UK): 00 353 1 6680400
Website: www.icai.ie

Institute of Chartered Accountants of Scotland (ICAS)
Chartered Accountants House, 21 Haymarket Yards, Edinburgh EH12 5BH
Tel: 0131 225 5673
Website: www.icas.org.uk

Institute of Chartered Secretaries and Administrators (ICSA)
16 Park Crescent, London W1N 4AH
Tel: 020 7580 4741
Website: www.icsa.org.uk

Index